Universal Laws

18 Powerful Laws & The Secret Behind Manifesting Your Desires

Finding Balance Series: Book 1

by Jennifer O'Neill, Spiritual Teacher

Universal Laws: 18 Powerful Laws & The Secret Behind Manifesting Your Desires
Copyright © 2013 by Jennifer O'Neill. All rights reserved.

Limitless Publishing, LLC
Kailua, HI 96734
www.limitlesspublishing.com

First Print Edition: May 2013
ISBN-13: 978-1-4848-3625-5
ISBN-10: 1-4848-3625-1

Cover: Eden Crane Designs
Formatting: Streetlight Graphics

No part of this book may be reproduced, scanned, or distributed in any printed or electronic form without permission. Please do not participate in or encourage piracy of copyrighted materials in violation of the author's rights. Thank you for respecting the hard work of this author.

Table of Contents

Introduction 5

What Are Universal Laws? 9

Universal Law #1
"The Law of One or Oneness" 12

Universal Law #2
"The Law of Vibration" 21

Universal Law #3
"The Law of Attraction" 27

Universal Law #4
"The Law of Allowing" 33

Universal Law #5
"The Law of Resistance" 41

Universal Law #6
"The Law of Detachment" 46

Universal Law #7
"The Law of Abundance" 54

Universal Law #8
"The Law of Intention" 60

Universal Law #9
"The Law of Action" 68

Universal Law #10
"The Law of Cause and Effect" 72

Universal Law #11
"The Law of Pure Potential" 79

Universal Law #12
"The Law of Rhythm or Ebb and Flow" 85

Universal Law #13
"The Law of Polarity" 90

Universal Law #14
"The Law of Relativity" 95

Universal Law #15
"The Law of Dharma or Purpose" 100

Universal Law #16
"The Law of Giving and Gratitude" 105

Universal Law #17
"The Law of Love" 109

Universal Law #18
"The Law of Correspondence" 115

What Does It "Feel" Like When Working
With Universal Laws & Manifestation? 118

Manifestation Exercises 123

Manifestation Meditation 129

Six Common Blocks That Keep You From
Manifesting Your Desires 131

About the Author 137

Other Books By Jennifer O'Neill 139

Introduction

When it comes to working with the Law of Attraction or manifesting your desires, there are many so called "secrets." When movies are produced or books are published on either of these two subjects, some of the most important information is, well, let's just say... "missing." You're only provided with half of the information that you need.

Is it on purpose? Maybe, sometimes...

Is it on accident? Probably, most of the time...

Is it because they don't know the entire truth themselves? Most likely...

This creates a huge problem for those of you who are interested in learning more about how to manifest your desires. Because you will *never, ever* be able to fully understand how to manifest things into your life without understanding how the ENTIRE process works.

Can you still manifest things into your life without understanding how the entire process works? Or more importantly WHY it works?

Of course! Will you be able to repeat the process without this knowledge? Or manifest a particular desire that you're focusing upon? Not likely. But here's the kicker—most people are "accidentally" manifesting things into their life all of the time. However, they're doing two things consistently, which are not doing them any favors:

• They're manifesting whatever it is they DON'T want to happen, (self-fulfilling prophecy).

• They're doing so without even realizing they're doing it!

This is definitely a problem!

I'm not sure how anyone expects other people to learn how to manifest their desires if they're only given part of the information. It's like you're setting them up to fail right off the bat, then they lose faith right away and think, "I knew it was too good to be true!" So what do they do? They go back to doing whatever it was they were doing in the first place—manifesting what they don't want to happen without even realizing it. This is something I wish to help you with. I want you to understand EXACTLY what it is that you're doing. I want to help you make sense of it all!

I want you to succeed!

I have taken this journey myself and the path that I've discovered has lead me to great success. But it wasn't always this way. I, like many others, had an easy time manifesting my desires up until I became a young adult, then…

I got married and had kids.

All of the sudden the world became a much scarier place. I began to worry about things I've never worried about before. *Things like money!* I needed it, and needed to make sure it was always available for food, heat, housing, clothing, and everything you would need to provide for your children. I also needed to be healthy! What would happen if I got sick or couldn't care for my children? I wanted to be able to care for them and watch them grow! Fear and panic set in…and my life was very different for the next ten years.

As my career as a psychic began to grow, something started to become very clear. I began to notice a very distinct pattern with clients and people who were around me.

They were their own worst enemy!

I don't mean in some regards, I mean in almost all regards. They caused themselves issues with:

- Career

- Love

- Money

Psychically it was very apparent, and yet the good thing was, I could always see a solution or a way out of this "problem mindset." It was easy because there were always two common factors which were dictating their future outcomes:

- Their thoughts of fear and worry.

- Their misunderstanding of how the world works around them.

There were very distinct patterns between these two things and what I would be shown (psychically) as the most probable future outcome for them. I knew this was something I should be paying very close attention to.

I began to see similarities in myself and how my "mindset" had also shifted over the years and I thought to myself, *how did this happen? When did this happen? I don't want to be like this anymore!* The good thing was, psychically, I was almost always shown an alternate future outcome. Kind of like when you read alternate ending books in which you can make different choices throughout the book and it essentially changes the outcome of the story. It's the same type of concept. So I began to work very closely with the Universal Laws again.

Fast forward to today. I'm having more fun working for myself than I ever thought possible, and I'm on track to make over six figures this year. I love helping people learn how to do what I do and teach them what I know, so I'll teach anyone who will listen. I love it when they finally "get it" and their lives begin to change.

However, this book is NOT for everyone!

Before you read this book:

1) You must have an open mind.

2) You must be willing to challenge your beliefs, and how you "think" the world currently works around you.

3) You must be okay with being different and *thinking* differently than those around you. You must be willing not to worry that they will "make fun of your new perspective" or "think you're crazy."

If you can learn to adapt a "who cares what anyone else thinks, I want a better life for myself" attitude, you'll be on the right track.

You must also understand that shifting your perspective won't happen overnight; it's a marathon, not a sprint. You'll need to learn how to "retrain" your brain and your subconscious to think differently. You'll need to learn how to see the world around you differently than you do now—this is a process. Most likely you've been trained (or what I like to call brainwashed) into thinking the world operates one way and one way only—the physical way—for your entire life up until this point.

Letting go of that belief is not always easy.

Did your parents and the people around you brainwash you on purpose? No. They truly thought life in this physical world was hard and they wanted to warn you and keep you from getting your hopes up.

But it does take time to *undo* this brainwashing and adhere to a new way of life, a way of finding balance—balance between the physical and spiritual world. If you are willing to learn what's in this book, then take this knowledge and integrate it into your everyday life, you will embark on the most rewarding journey of your life…

What Are Universal Laws?

In order for you to understand how the manifestation process works in its entirety, it's important for you to have a general understanding of the Universal Laws. You don't need to memorize them or even know each one completely, however, there are some very key points which you must learn. These key points will help you make sense of why it all works the way it does. They will help you understand what formula lies behind the manifestation process. So what are Universal Laws exactly?

Everything in existence has a physical and spiritual component to them. Here are some characteristics of a physical component:

• A physical component consists of mass and matter, primarily things which most people can *see and touch*, such as furniture, trees, houses, cars, water, etcetera.

• **Physical components are dictated by what are called Physical Laws, such as the Law of Gravity and the Law of Motion.**

• Most people are somewhat familiar with these laws, because these subjects are touched upon when you attend school. It's important for you to understand such laws and how the physical world around us operates.

Here are some characteristics of a spiritual component:

• A spiritual component primarily deals with energy.

• Energy is something you can *feel* with your spiritual body, but many times it remains undetectable to the naked eye.

• **Spiritual components are dictated by what we call Universal Laws.**

- Since Universal Laws primarily deal with all things energy related, such as intention and action, and things you *cannot see,* people tend to dismiss their validity.

- It wasn't until the very popular Law of Attraction became a household name that Universal Laws were no longer considered less valuable in the physical world. All of a sudden, there was some validity to Universal Laws. In fact, they became important!

How do they become laws?

These laws are "conclusions" based on many, many years of repeated experiments and observations, thus being universally accepted into the scientific community as a law.

Universal Laws are laws that dictate the way in which Universal Energy behaves.

- *Quantum physics has been able to make more of a breakthrough in this area than any of the other Sciences.*

Why should any of this matter to you?

Because it makes your life a whole lot easier when you understand Universal Laws, just as it does when you understand Physical Laws. You would not walk to the edge of a cliff, step off of the edge, and expect to float there, since you have no desire to fall to the ground below. Why? Because you understand the Law of Gravity and the Law of Gravity is a Physical Law. Physical Laws apply to you while you are here on earth experiencing life in the physical realm, therefore, you will hit the ground below if you step off of the edge of the cliff. Having this information is very helpful to you and disaster is averted!

This is also why it's important to become familiar with Universal Laws. You are a spiritual being, even while having a physical experience. As spiritual beings, Universal Laws will dictate the behavior of Universal Energy, which also makes up a part of your own existence, as well as other Universal Energy you might encounter and work with on a daily basis. That's a fact. As spiritual and energetic beings, your experience is being dictated by Universal Laws every day, whether you are aware of it or not, just as it is by Physical Laws. It will affect your love life and it most definitely will affect your money flow. In order to help you live the best life possible, I would like to introduce you to the eighteen Universal Laws.

"Insanity is doing the same thing over and over again and expecting different results."

—**Albert Einstein**

Universal Law #1
"The Law of One or Oneness"

The Law of One or Oneness—Everything is connected, we are all one.

This is a really great law that will help open the doors to understanding all of the other Universal Laws.

The Law of One or Oneness dictates that we are all one and everything is connected.

• Everything is part of a greater whole.

• More commonly, people refer to this greater whole as source, or energy, and in many instances, God.

• As part of a greater whole, everything you can *see* as well as the things you *can't see* are all dictated by the same Universal Energy, and therefore, by Universal Laws.

How can this be?

Because everything is made up of Universal Energy, coming from the same energetic source.

UNIVERSAL LAWS

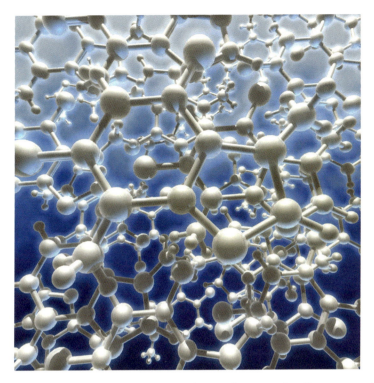

Four Important Things to Remember When You're Learning About The Law of One or Oneness:

• All of the things you can see and all of the things you can't see just "appear" to take on different forms, shapes, or sizes. Things such as tables, chairs, thoughts, people, all of these things are made up of Universal Energy.

• Most likely, with your current mindset, you'll see and view all of these things as very separate components from one another (not interconnected as they truly are in the grand scheme of things). Visually they appear to be so different from one another in your mind with all of these different forms, shapes, sizes, and even colors, that it makes it hard for your mind to *understand* how everything is connected, or how one thing will affect another.

• When you view all of the things in your life that way, *as separate and individual components*, it makes Universal Laws seem very confusing at best, and impossible at worst.

- You need to "retrain" your brain in order to understand and accept that the world around you is not how it appears to be. This isn't even metaphysics, this is scientific fact!

When you break it all down, *everything is the same, everything is energy.*

I'm sure you've heard of atoms or molecules before. You can't see them, but you know everything is made of them. It's the same type of concept; everything is energy coming from the same source. Since we are all one, each individual thing having an affect on all of the other things in your existence is a lot easier than you think. It's like a chain reaction.

How might The Law of One or Oneness affect love or your love life?

Love is just like everything else, it can be attracted and it can be repelled…it's energy.

You should never view love as something separate from yourself or who you are, it's a part of you and it enhances who you are. There's love flowing through everything; love is a part of a greater whole. When your perception of love is that it's something separate from who you are, or from your life, then it becomes so.

It becomes law.

Let's take Nicole, for instance. She's a very successful woman on the outside, but on the inside she feels very lonely and really wants a relationship in her life. She's had a few long-term relationships come and go over the years; she's even been married once before. But the lack of love in her life has been an issue for a while, even when she was in past relationships. Love is something that she's always felt she was lacking from her partners in the past. Now she's afraid that she'll never experience the love she's looking for in a future relationship, either. What is happening?

Nicole views love as something separate from herself.

Something she's lacking in her life. Love, in her perception, is something she receives from outside of herself. So in this case, Universal Law dictates that *love is lacking.*

This is like a catch twenty-two. *When someone feels as if love is lacking in their life, they tend to focus very hard (unintentionally) upon not feeling love.* They'll focus very hard on love being absent. To fill this void, they will do what most people are taught, they will search for love coming from somewhere else, from somewhere outside of himself or herself, usually from another person. The problem with doing this is:

When you separate love from who you are and view it as a separate entity, more often than not, you will repel it.

People are always picking up on "energetic signs and signals" from other people who they come into contact with. Any thoughts you have regarding love will become a thought pattern which then translates as a "vibe" that you're sending out into the Universe. Here are some examples of thought patterns which become instant love repellers:

Why don't I have a boyfriend/girlfriend?

Where are they all?

I'm so lonely.

Everyone else has love in their life. What about me?

Imagine as if all of your thoughts or *feelings* are transmitted out into the world as an energetic telegraph. Imagine this telegraph going out into the world giving a message to all of the people you come into contact with. What happens is, the people who you come into contact with (who won't know why), will receive a signal (or feeling) indicating that you're unapproachable.

Here's what happens:

- *They can feel desperation or neediness emitting from you because they're also apart of the greater whole.*

- Your perception or thought pattern indicating "love is separate from who I am" will instead isolate you from the love you are so desperately searching for.

- You will consciously hold yourself outside of the greater whole in your own little isolation booth that you have energetically created.

How might you resolve this issue?

- *First, you must acknowledge that love comes from within, not from outside of yourself, not even from another person.*

- That feeling of "love" you think you receive from other people? *That feeling comes from inside of your body and from inside of your chest, from YOU.* That feeling does not permeate your being from the outside and make its way in.

Think of it this way. Have you ever had someone express his or her "love" for you, but you didn't feel the same way back? If you didn't feel the same way back, it's because love is a part of you and who you are. It comes from deep inside of your soul, someone else can't just throw it upon you and all of a sudden you're in love.

Love emits from you, from the inside.

Once you understand this, you will begin to emit love more often and your heart chakra will open. You will begin to love more, just to feel the goodness of love. There will be no strings attached, no ulterior motives, just love. These things cause your perception of love to alter a bit. You will feel it more, you will give it more, and you will receive it more!

The way the Law of One or Oneness works with money is also very similar. Money is energy coming from the same source.

Let me repeat that ... Money is ENERGY coming from the same source!

You're a part of money and money is a part of you. Before you roll your eyes here, just give it a minute to sink in. We are all part of one, we are all energy, we are all under the same rules, and we are all part of everything.

Some people have a perception of money as something so sought after, so limited, and so hard to get, that it's not only separate from them and who they are, but it's really hard to come by.

Three Important Things You Need to Learn When it Comes to Money:

1) Money's not untouchable.

Money's not something that's only for the special people, and money's not a reward for something done right.

2) Money IS energy.

It is energy (currency) that circulates (or is in circulation). As energy, it continuously flows in and out of our lives daily, (unless it's redirected), and it will continue to circulate throughout the Universe. If you ever listen to some of the richest people in the world talk about money, or any of the very popular financial advisors, they understand money in its truest form. They consistently refer to money as an energy or currency, not an object that you possess.

3) Money comes from the same source as you.

When money becomes separate from you and who you are, or when anything becomes separate from who you are, it becomes less attainable. Your perspective often shifts to, "There it is, it needs to be had or attained. In order to obtain it, I must do XYZ."

Imagine this for a minute; let's pretend that money is a part of your family. You see it often, you can ask it to help you do things, you can invite it places and it will show up. There's a mutual respect between the two of you and it's a part of your "family" (coming from the same source). You know it will always be in your life, how often it shows up, however, is really up to you.

Now imagine a different story. Imagine that money is a stranger. You don't come from the same source and money has absolutely no reason to do anything that you ask. There's no mutual respect between the two of you. You never see money, so it doesn't matter if it shows up or not.

In fact, you so rarely see it that you're not even surprised at it's scarcity.

Do you see the difference?

Do you FEEL the difference?

Money is not a stranger from a different source with an agenda that's only serving the worthy.

Money is a part of the same source as you, money is energy! As energy, money is attracted, it's directed, and can be repelled. If you don't view money as part of a greater whole, as part of an energy flow, then most likely you (unknowingly) view it as separate from who you are. When that happens, it becomes harder to obtain and you'll begin to isolate yourself from money.

When you view money as part of your existence and view it as attainable, it is.

• **The rich have a very different perception of money.**

• You know the saying the rich get richer and the poor get poorer? The rich feel they are worthy of having money, because they're in the same family, they view it as very attainable…they view it as a "part" of who

UNIVERSAL LAWS

they are. Did you catch that? Most wealthy people truly feel like money is a "part" of them and a part of who they are. In fact, they strongly identify themselves with money.

- *It's a part of their very own identity!*

When you view money separate from yourself and hard to obtain, it is.

- **People who are struggling with money, on the other hand, feel that money is not a part of them at all.**

- They feel the very opposite of the rich. Not only do they feel they're not made of money, but they rarely see money.

- It's very much separate from who they are and their lifestyle.

- *They view money as hard to obtain.*

Most people like to make the argument of, "Well, it's easy for the rich to feel that way about money because they've always had money." Not true.

Did you know approximately eighty-six percent of today's millionaires were not wealthy growing up? **They are self-made millionaires.**

What sets them apart, however, is their view or perception about money. "It is and always will be attainable…"

Universal Law #2
"The Law of Vibration"

The Law of Vibration—Everything in the Universe vibrates, or offers a vibration.

This is a *very* important law, so pay close attention to this chapter. The Law of Vibration is very closely linked with The Law of Attraction. If you are, or ever have been struggling with The Law of Attraction, understanding this law will help you immensely.

The Law of Vibration dictates that everything in the Universe has a vibration or a vibrational frequency.

• People, thoughts, or things all offer a vibration.

• The vibration of physical things like your television or your couch, vibrate on a molecular level. In other words, don't stare at your couch too long in hopes that you can see it move or vibrate, as you'll need special equipment to see this happening. Just know all things vibrate.

• Vibration is much more easily detectible in people, and as spiritual beings, you're actually equipped to sense it with your spiritual senses.

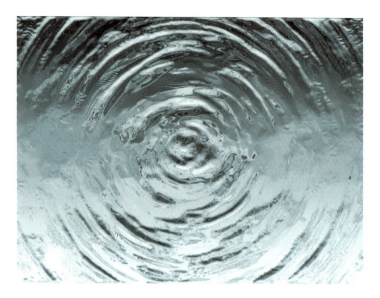

Why is it important for you to understand The Law of Vibration? Because you work with this law every day and it has a huge impact on your life.

Imagine for a minute that you're a giant human magnet. The strength of your magnet depends upon each individual person. Your magnet can be very powerful, or it can be very weak. What dictates the strength of your magnet? One very particular thing…

Your mood!

That's right, your mood. As a person (who was energetically created) imagine you're always vibrating somewhere on a scale between one and ten. When you're sad, upset, depressed, or worried, energetically this means you're vibrating very low on the scale, somewhere around a one, two, or a three at best. When you're very happy, laughing, and truly enjoying yourself, The Law of Vibration dictates you're vibrating very high, around a seven, eight, or a nine, with ten being the highest you can go.

The lower your vibration, the less powerful your magnet is. The higher your vibration, the more powerful your magnet becomes. When you're working with a powerful magnet, the quicker you draw things into your life and the quicker The Law of Attraction will respond.

Happiness = Higher vibration and therefore a powerful magnet

Sadness = Lower vibration and therefore a weak magnet

How might The Law of Vibration affect your love life? It's really very simple…

• *People prefer to be around other people who offer a higher vibration, always.*

• People who offer a higher vibration tend to be happier people, they like to laugh, they seem secure with themselves, they have a positive outlook on life and really cool things always seem happen to them!

• When you are around people who offer a higher vibration they will also naturally uplift your own vibration. They will pull your vibration upward, and it *feels* good!

Many times people don't like to be around other people who offer a lower vibration because they tend to be:

• Sad, depressed, tired, and hopeless.

• Low vibration people have a negative outlook on life and this can feel like an energetic weight pulling you down.

- Another aspect of low vibration people is they can be very draining. Do you ever notice sometimes when you're around certain people they can be extremely exhausting? So much so, that when you're no longer in their presence you just feel like taking a nap? We call these people "Energy Vampires" in the psychic world. They tend to suck as much energy as they can from other people to help them maintain even a low vibration, because it takes a lot of energy to keep a consistently low vibration.

Isn't that weird? It actually takes more energy to keep a low vibration than it does to maintain a high vibration.

Tip#1

For Those Who Are Looking For Love

As a human magnet, like vibrations attract each other, so you have to be very careful if you're offering a lower vibration of what type of people or significant others you may be drawing into your life. You want your vibration to be the best it can be, because low vibration people are a lot of work. If you get into a relationship with one, it can be frustrating and exhausting to say the least. The best thing to do is figure out where you naturally tend to hang out vibrationally on the scale. Are you mostly vibrating at a five and below or a five and above? If you're mostly vibrating at a five and above, you're good, no worries here. However, if you're mostly vibrating at five and below, well, you have some work to do. You can get into a relationship sure enough, but most likely you'll draw into your life another person who is of a lower vibration (sad, depressed, not happy). Not the best foundation for a relationship.

Tip #2

For Those Who Are In A Relationship

People will change vibrations at different points in their life, so all is good if you're both high vibration people. Will you have your low days? Sure. It's natural to move up and down the scale. But when you throw someone who's mostly a low vibration person into the mix, then it can become an issue. The key is really to become aware of the vibration of the people you surround yourself with most often and learn how to deal with it the best you can, as not to let it affect your own vibration. I have written a lot more on this subject in my book "Energy Vampires: How to Deal With Negative People."

How does The Law of Vibration affect your life when it comes to money?

It will really affect your money flow on several different levels. As a human magnet, you want to attract money into your life, you don't want to repel it. How do you do this? Happiness equals higher vibration and therefore a powerful magnet. The higher your vibration, the more powerful your magnet becomes. When you're working with a powerful magnet, the quicker you draw things into your life and the quicker The Law of Attraction will respond.

Money is no longer the goal…happiness is!

Happiness will affect your money flow. If you tend to be offering a low vibration, many times you become stuck in a poverty mindset. What's a poverty mindset? A poverty mindset is something like this: *You're certain that all things related to money are driven by the economy and the economy is bad, so you are doomed to be poor!*

For example, do you ever find yourself thinking any of these things?

• I've always struggled in the past. I am struggling now, and I don't see how it's ever going to change.

• There are not enough jobs out there. Since no one else is getting hired, I know that I won't, either.

• I can never afford anything I want!

• Those people that live like that are different and they have better skills. I never get a break!

• I want to do XYZ but I'll never be able to because I don't see it getting any better for me.

- The economy is screwed, that means so am I!

It's so important for you to get this, and I really mean get this:

1) Your thoughts DO become a reality and your vibration *magnifies* The Law of Attraction to a whole different level.

It makes your thoughts powerful beyond belief! This is not metaphysics, this is quantum physics and it's been proven on a scientific level. When working with the premise that your thoughts do become reality, what do you think these types of thoughts will do to your money flow? Let's just say it's not going to do you any favors.

2) There are more people making more money, every second, of every day, than you can possibly imagine!

Now if it's just (physical) law that everyone's finances are dictated by the economy, then this would not be possible. It doesn't add up. Which brings us to our next point.

3) There's something more out there that dictates our money flow.

Money is energy, energy is directed by Universal Laws. This is something which you might have heard before, but most likely have never been *taught* before.

It involves retraining your brain and your subconscious, which, let's face it, can be very hard to do as we can be very stubborn at times. Tearing down all of your preconceived notions of what you thought you knew about money and *reprogramming* your mind to think differently than you've been taught thus far and to think differently than those around you…

It's not easy, but it can be done, I did it and you can to.

Universal Law #3
"The Law of Attraction"

The Law of Attraction—You attract into your life what you are offering vibrationally.

This law is the most popular of all the Universal Laws. It's been a focus in the last several years because it has a very magical feel to it, which in my opinion, makes it all the more intriguing. The problem with this Law, unfortunately, is it's not properly understood.

The Law of Attraction dictates that you will "attract" into your life whatever you are offering "vibrationally."

• All things vibrate (The Law of Vibration) and everything offers a vibration, which is directly tied to The Law of Attraction.

• Your mood and your belief system are both very powerful components when it comes to utilizing The Law of Attraction.

• *Visualizing is **only** to be used as a TOOL to help shift your mood and belief system, so your vibration and what you're offering vibrationally shifts.*

• It's not to be used as "the key component" to visualize what you're wishing to attract, and poof it appears! Visualizing is NOT your magic lamp.

• Most people don't properly understand The Law of Attraction. What people *think* it means is you will attract into your life what it is that you think about or concentrate the hardest on (magic lamp theory). This is where many people get confused.

When you're working with Universal Laws, you're working with Universal Energy. As spiritual beings we're very powerful energetically, and this Universal Energy is attached to our spiritual bodies. Universal Energy manifests itself into forming *our reality* by how we are *feeling* to the very depths of our soul.

For instance, let's say you concentrate very hard on getting a bigger house or getting a better paying job. But deep down you're still in disbelief that these things could actually become a part of your reality.

• **Disbelief, unfortunately, in this instance, is what you're offering vibrationally.**

• Your emotions and how you feel about something or someone, in this case disbelief, is what *actually* dictates your vibration (as we discussed in the previous chapter), visualizing does not.

Take a neutral perspective for a minute and forget everything you thought you knew about The Law of Attraction, and look at it like this.

Visualizing bigger house + disbelief = I strongly disbelieve that I will ever have a bigger house.

You don't stand a chance! You're just concreting this belief into the Universe that a bigger house is not meant for you. You may be wondering:

"Why doesn't visualizing allow me to offer what I want vibrationally?"

"When I'm concentrating on something becoming a reality, why doesn't that work?"

"Why am I being taught to visualize in the first place, then?"

This should help answer any of those questions.

Three Important Reasons To Visualize:

• Although visualizing is not what holds the energetic universal power, visualizing is still an important and valuable component. Visualizing is meant to be used as a tool to trigger an emotional response within yourself. These emotions then dictate your vibration.

• More often than not when you visualize something, you cannot usually do so without it causing some type of emotional response. Whether it's a good feeling or a bad feeling, some type of feeling is usually "triggered" and attached to whatever it is that you are thinking about.

• *This emotional response is where all the power lies!*

What you need to learn how to do is to *conjure up positive feelings* about whatever it is that you're visualizing. You need to learn how to truly believe it's possible. When you can master those things, you will take The Law of Attraction to a whole new level.

Visualizing bigger house + belief, "I have always known I am meant to have a bigger house" = bigger house!

When you're stuck with disbelief, you must find a way to trick yourself into believing anything's possible. Find a way to feel the possibilities, find a way to feel a positive outcome. When you can figure that out, then you will truly understand how The Law of Attraction works. It only takes truly believing in something one time, and seeing it happen the way you wish it to, to flip your perception in the right direction. Because when it happens, it's amazing! Although it's kind of like a catch twenty-two, you have to trust and believe first, and then it happens, not the other way around.

How The Law of Attraction affects your love life is quite interesting. It really comes down to one thing:

What do you truly believe about men or what do you truly believe about women?

If you're a man and you *believe* women are out to stomp on your heart, or they're untrustworthy, but you continue to date, thinking, "There must be some good women out there, if I date enough, I should certainly find one." *What's your true belief here?*

Visualizing a significant other + (belief) women stomp on your heart = heart stomping relationship.

You can't win this way; The Law of Attraction dictates a heart stomping. If you're a woman and you *believe* that most all men are unfaithful or noncommittal, but some of your friends are in relationships with good guys, so there must be a few stragglers out there.

Visualizing a significant other + (belief) men are unfaithful or noncommittal = no long-term relationship.

Although there was a glimmer of hope in both perspectives, the dominant vibration will take over.

• Whatever feeling is the strongest will dominate over all of the other feelings, it will become Alpha.

• And there can only be one Alpha.

So if you're thinking, "But I can always find some glimmer of hope to match what I am visualizing." This is probably why you have been unsuccessful, because the Alpha feeling doesn't match up.

Now that may sound heavy, but it's not!

How are you feeling on the inside in this instant?

What you are energetically manifesting?

Let's take the house scenario again. Do you feel like a bigger house is a possibility somehow, some way, because things that you've always wanted in the past have ended up finding a way to you?

What about jobs? Do you feel like there are millions of jobs out in the world, and there's most certainly at least a few that pay well, which you are equally qualified for?

Feel the alignment energetically by "visualizing and feeling a better scenario"?

Or do you feel like this:

- "Money's tight and everyone's struggling, so getting a bigger house is a pipe dream, but I am going to do my best to visualize it."

- "There are no jobs in this town, I am lucky to have the job I do have."

- "No one I know gets paid much at all. But I will visualize a better job, so I can get a bigger house."

Do you see the difference? *Do you FEEL the contradiction in energy?*

There's no alignment. There's only disbelief, worry, and fear. So you can visualize all you want to, but if you don't feel that it's a possibility, then you have resistance to it becoming a reality (The Law of Resistance). You end up putting up your own blockers, or energetic blocks.

Now here's the crazy thing…

Why is it so easy for people to believe in a negative outcome and so hard for them to believe in a positive outcome?

When did it even become your belief that life is supposed to be hard? That money is hard to come by? When did that happen? Think about it for minute. It was taught to you. You weren't born into the world thinking that life was hard and money was so important that you have to grasp at it every chance you get. When you were little, you didn't even care about money! You just wanted to fill your day doing whatever it was that you enjoyed doing the most.

Then as you began to get older, your belief system was formed. That's most likely when you were taught how hard life is.

• You are taught you must go to college to make a living and if you choose any other route you are doomed to be poor.

• You are taught everybody struggles, that's just life.

• You are taught only certain jobs make money, that's just the way things work.

• You are taught if you pursue anything creative such as music, art, or writing you will struggle your whole life.

• ***You are taught that there are only a few lucky ones and you are not one of them...***

It doesn't take long for this thought process to become your reality. Observing your parents, your family, and friends also helps to form your belief system. Watching them and how they struggle with money makes it real. They were also taught these very same things as children.

It can be very different, however, if you are aware enough and determined enough to convince yourself anything is possible. People buy bigger houses every day, why can't it be you? People fall in love every day, why can't it be you? People get better jobs every day, why can't it be you?

Somehow, someway, it will happen. Because anything is a possible (The Law of Pure Potential) and there is plenty to go around (The Law of Abundance).

Universal Law #4
"The Law of Allowing"

The Law of Allowing—allowing things to move without resistance and to evolve and grow naturally.

This is one of my most favorite laws and I think one of the most important Universal Laws. Most people really struggle with this one, however, since we've been trained to think differently for most of our lives.

The Law of Allowing dictates that all Universal Energy runs in currents and these currents have a flow to them.

• When you allow the Universal flow to evolve and grow naturally, things will begin to manifest in a fluid non-chaotic manner.

• You are allowing the Universe to create and manifest freely with no interference.

• This law feels the most *unnatural* to most people because our brain is not "trained" to allow. We've been trained to think that *allowing is being lazy.*

• **The state of allowing is the purest state of manifesting.**

This law is really, really hard for people to wrap their minds around. Many times we (as people living a physical existence) have been trained to believe we must try and take control of every situation in order to control the outcome of what it is we desire. We have been taught to believe that without our guidance or control, things will not happen in the way we wish them to.

We must control our destiny!

The problem with this perspective and needing to have control is you're under the impression that you know what the best possible outcome is. I hate to break the news to you, but you do not...

We are children of the Universe, and while we have our own ideas of how we *think* things must be done and in what order, Momma always knows best. The reason we can't make this determination is because there's such an abundance of ways in which the outcome we desire can take place, and many of them you don't even know about! Many times the outcome the Universe has in mind is much better than the outcome we have dreamt up for ourselves. *How can this be?* You may wonder. It's really fairly simple...

We do not have enough information to determine the best possible outcome for our desires.

We usually base our desired outcome on our physical perspective. From a physical perspective, our perspective is usually *extremely* limited. We are like kindergartners trying to access our desires.

So how do you work with this law?

• By accepting that you don't always know the best possible outcome.

• By realizing that control is only an *illusion* and you will never be able to control anything, any situation, or anyone without consent. In actuality, there is no control, there's only consent.

• By being open to what might come your way.

• By learning to let go of control and allow things to develop and unfold naturally for you the way they are supposed to.

Imagine there's an abundance of Universal Energy, which is in constant creation. This energy is in constant flow, continuously creating and manifesting an infinite number of things at every given moment in time. The world and the people in it are a blank canvas to this Universal Energy, and when you allow this flow to create and manifest with it's own vision in mind, something amazing happens.

This energy seems to be able to merge with your most intimate desires and manifest them right before your eyes!

It's amazing how all things become so carefully orchestrated that it allows everything to fall into place so precisely. It's as if you are watching the most incredible artistic flow you've ever seen, manifesting itself into a physical state.

However, when you're unaware of The Law of Allowing, *fear* tends to drive your thoughts and you begin working with The Law of Resistance (next chapter), which is a law that is *fear driven.*

This can most definitely cause an issue with your love life. What's the number one concern of most people when it comes to love?

It's the fear of being alone.

Oddly enough, this fear affects most people. It affects people who are single, for obvious reasons. They're currently alone and don't wish to stay that way. But it also very much affects people who are in unhappy or are in unfulfilling relationships.

More importantly, it affects the choices people may otherwise make if it wasn't for the fear of being alone.

This fear can and will affect The Law of Allowing.

People tend to make very bad choices based on fear and force themselves to stay in or choose relationships which are neither healthy nor a good fit for them. For instance, thought patterns based on fear go like this:

- "This relationship is so hard, but we've been together forever, and I hate to throw it all away."

- "We fight so much, but when we get along, it's really great."

- "I think it's best to stay together for the kids."

- "This is what marriage is supposed to be like, no point in doing it all over again."

These are all thoughts based on the fear of being alone. When misery is more tolerable than the thought of being alone, it's really pretty sad. When you force yourself to stay in a situation (love or otherwise), which feels like such a struggle, even when you can choose a different route… well, that's definitely **the opposite of The Law of Allowing.** It's like trying to wrestle the paintbrush out of the Universe's hand so you can paint a picture of what it is you want or what it is you think you want.

The problem is your dominant or alpha thought:

- "I'm not happy in this relationship."

- "I'm miserable with this person."

- "Relationships suck!"

Basically, if you do win the wrestling match, you're really going to be putting graffiti on your wall, and not the pretty kind.

So stop resisting, don't be afraid of being alone!

Trust in the flow and the creative power of the Universe, of something bigger than you. Trust in the notion that you deserve happiness in everything you do, relationships and otherwise. *Trust that out of 7.5 billion people, there's a very happy person out in the world you are meant to be with!*

Part of the trust factor with The Law of Allowing stems from the belief that there's only a limited amount of things in the world and all good things are already taken, or untouchable by you. Universal Law dictates this is not true on both accounts.

Unless…you believe it to be true. (Ahhh, those catch twenty-two's).

Here's what I mean:

Physical perspective—

You've been taught for so many years how fact is just fact, based on math. How things are not magical and how Santa Claus is not real. How life is hard and don't expect it to be anything different. Thought patterns such as:

• "They only print so much money. The earth only has so many resources, this is scientific fact!"

• "There are only XYZ jobs available in my town, and there are ABC people looking for jobs. You do the math!"

• "How in the world is it possible for me to get out of my current debt? I have a ton of debt and not enough income coming in to make a dent in it. I just don't see it happening."

Now based on what you've been taught and what you based your knowledge of how you think the world works around you and how money is obtained, naturally The Law of Allowing would seem silly based on this perspective. There's just simply not enough money, jobs, etcetera to serve everyone. So therefore, control is the alternative, so you think.

Universal perspective—

Some people never truly believed these things they were taught, because there's also a bazillion instances of people who live quite amazing lives, people who statistically should not (according to the math and other things they've been taught thus far), and so they've decided those things must not be true.

• These people work quite nicely with The Law of Allowing.

• *They will find their groove with the purest state of manifesting, just because they don't share the same view as the rest of the world!*

Amazing, isn't it? They don't resist the notion of money, jobs, or material things being in their reach, because their internal view is different. Anything they desire is reachable.

Anything is possible, anything is allowable!

They don't resist the notion of where they can make an income, or how things might work out well for them, despite what everyone else says or thinks. They think things like:

• "Well, they need someone for this job, why not me? I'm qualified!"

• "There's lots of people in the world making over 100K a year even in this economic downturn, not everyone is poor."

• "Some people I know are doing quite well in life, they're adaptable, and so am I!"

Think about this for a minute. Let's say there's an abundance of money (The Law of Abundance), a never-ending supply of it. And this never-ending supply is a river that flows by you at all times.

UNIVERSAL LAWS

All you need to do is to allow some of it to flow into your world and not resist it (by putting up a barrier, or energetic dam around you), with the notion that it's true and some of it belongs in your world.

This may sound weird, but your relationship with money works in a very similar manner as your relationship with people.

What is your thought process when it comes to money?

• "It's not around much, but when it is, we have a good time."

• "I will take what I can get." (Low standards when it comes to what you can get.)

• "It's always a struggle and it will always be a struggle, that's just how it is."

What's your dominant or alpha thought?

(You're taught) Money's hard to come by and there's a limited supply + (belief) I don't *see* how it's possible to be financially secure = No Money!

You don't have to see to believe it...

Believe in something more powerful than what you can see.

Believe in something bigger than you.

Believe in something ... DIFFERENT than everyone else believes to be true!

Do not follow the masses and resist a better life just because others have told you it's not out there. If everyone did that, there would be no breakthroughs in the medical industry, there would be no spiritual development, or even past discoveries in the history of the world. Things would never get better for anyone!

Stop resisting change, stop thinking you know better.

Trust in the Universe and in the laws that dictate all things. Allow things to fall into place for you *just once*, and see what happens.

Universal Law #5
"The Law of Resistance"

The Law of Resistance—Anything offering resistance will manifest itself into energy blockages or stuck energy.

I feel this law is one of the most complicated and confusing laws. Most everyone struggles with this law at some point in his or her life. The key is to be able to recognize when it's happening and understand that it may be causing you some difficulty.

The Law of Resistance is a manifestation of energy in the state of resistance.

• This law is practiced most often without you being consciously aware you are working with this law.

• Universal Law, specifically The Law of Attraction, dictates energetically things move towards what's energetically prominent at the time, like a magnet. Like energy seeks out like energy. The Law of Resistance results in manifesting energy which is forceful and negative in nature.

• When energy is negative, or forceful in nature, it will disrupt the natural flow of energy. The current or river which is being disrupted will result in stuck energy or blockages.

The more resistant you are to an outcome, the faster you will create an abundance of stuck energy or blockages. This allows the outcome to which you're so resistant to pull up and park itself right smack in the middle of your world! Energy takes longer to clear out when it's stuck and blocking your way. It makes things harder; it's like an energetic traffic jam.

Imagine it like this, let's say that you feel forced to take a road trip from one destination to another. Instead of being able the take the route you wish to take, that route is closed for repairs, so you are detoured and forced to take an alternate route. What happens when people feel forced to take alternate routes to their planned destination? Usually one of two things:

1) **Adaption.**

Some people will adapt to this unexpected detour and go with the flow. They may or may not be excited about it, but they will adapt nonetheless. They are open to what lies ahead, and therefore, they're not resistant to it. They may find themselves thinking things like:

• "I've never been this way before, this might be fun."

• "This is unexpected. I would've preferred to go the other way, but maybe I will experience something new."

• "I'm not super excited about this, but there must be a reason for it... so I guess we'll see what it is!"

UNIVERSAL LAWS

When your thought process is along these lines, what happens is you begin to work with The Law of Allowing. You open up your energetic highway instead of creating a traffic jam (blocked or stuck energy) clogging up the highway. Instead of freaking out and becoming fearful and afraid, you manage to see things through the eyes of adventure or newness.

This allows the road ahead of you to stay clear and allows your energetic highway to flow with ease.

On the other hand, there are people who have a great deal of trouble adapting, so they tend to take another route, which brings us to number two.

2) Resistance.

Some people become so uncomfortable and so fearful when things change unexpectedly that they don't adapt well at all. In fact, they become very resistant. They're afraid things won't turn out the way they wish them to, they're afraid of being uncomfortable, and they are afraid of not being in control. They find themselves thinking things like:

- "This is terrible! Things are not going well."

- "What's happening? I knew this was going to happen."

- "Nothing ever turns out right!"

People who usually find themselves in a state of resistance are people who usually feel the need to control things in their life. They have placed an expectation on something because they want to *control* the outcome. Herein lies the problem. *When an expectation is placed, there's resistance to any other outcome than what is expected.* They've decided this is the only acceptable outcome (otherwise, there would be no expectation.)

An expectation is a *belief* that there will be a certain outcome in the future, which may or may not be realistic. A *belief* is when you have faith or confidence, that something is fact or true, without substantial proof. Expectations usually involve another person, or people, or an outcome of a situation, oftentimes resulting in disappointment. Wow! I bet you never realized how complicated having an expectation could be.

Expectations are extremely toxic to your happiness and therefore, affect what you're offering vibrationally and what you're manifesting into your life. (The Law of Vibration = what you will attract, aka The Law of Attraction).

Problems with expectations:

#1 Element of control

When people have placed an expectation on someone or something, it's usually because they want to *control* what the outcome essentially is. When an expectation is placed, there's *resistance* to any other outcome than what is expected. You've decided this is the only acceptable outcome (otherwise, there would be no expectation.)

#2 Belief

Belief means that you believe there will be a certain outcome in the future, which may or may not be realistic without substantial proof! The crazy thing about this is you have no substantial proof that things are going to turn out the way you expect them to, yet you are still expecting it to turn out the way in which you believe it will. One of the greatest things about the future is that the future is constantly changing. However, that also makes it hard to anticipate a certain outcome.

#3 Disappointment

When you become rigid in your thinking, you have a very high probability of disappointment. The act of feeling disappointment itself is not the whole problem, but the resistance that you feel in the body as a result of acquiring an expectation is. Resistance and other negative feelings felt energetically in the body, such as disappointment, can and do cause illness.

We did address these things in the previous chapter on The Law of Allowing as the two laws do tend be closely related.

The Law of Resistance can be one of the hardest laws to learn to master.

Many times it seems to be a constant wrestling match between your mind and Universal Law in a battle of wills as you try and wrestle with it to force a certain outcome. But wrestling with any Universal Law is like trying to wrestle with water…it will get you nowhere. It's a lot more effective and much less exhausting when you learn to stop resisting. When you can learn to float with the Universal current whichever way it's taking you. After you do it a few times you will learn that you will arrive at your destination eventually. So it's best to relax and take in the scenery along the way!

Universal Law #6
"The Law of Detachment"

The Law of Detachment—This is the law of releasing or letting go of your desire.

I find this law is one of the most freeing laws you will ever work with! It's not simple, but it's definitely worth the effort. If you can shift your perspective in such a way that you can work with The Law of Detachment, the other laws will fall right into place like dominos.

The Law of Detachment dictates that you must maintain a certain level of detachment when working with manifestation.

• When you maintain a certain amount of detachment to what it is you desire, you will allow that very thing to manifest itself into your existence.

• **The Law of Detachment must be active in order for The Law of Allowing to work, (the purest state of manifesting).**

• *One of the most importing things about The Law of Detachment is it keeps you from charging a thought negatively.*

How your thoughts are *charged* is really important when you are working with Universal Laws and manifestation.

In essence, it has the most impact on determining the outcome of what it is you desire. What exactly happens when you think about a particular outcome or manifestation?

• Your thoughts or energy waves, which you send out into the Universe (knowingly or unknowingly), become charged with a powerful emotion.

• When you *charge* a thought with a positive feeling or positive emotion, the outcome is excellent. (This is much more easily done when you have detached yourself from a specific outcome.)

• When you *charge* a thought with a fear, worry, or negative emotion, well, the outcome is not so great. (This is often done when you are attached to a particular outcome.)

Why does this happen? How do we end up charging a thought negatively? Most of us over the years have been taught and trained to believe all good things do not come easily, if and when things turn out good at all! It's been told to us for so long that our brain goes on autopilot in a sense, and we're not even paying attention to it. When you are afraid and worried, it's natural to grasp onto something, anything which might make you feel better, or not so anxious. So naturally we try and see an outcome which eases the anxiety, and then attach ourselves to that vision. Which is great if you can remain detached from a particular outcome. But what happens when you become attached to a particular outcome or manifestation?

• Fear begins to take over. You become afraid of things turning out badly, unless it happens the way you planned (the outcome you have become attached to).

• Your thoughts will then be charged negatively with a negative (or fear based) emotion and you'll worry that things will not turn out the way you wish them to.

Negative emotions work wonderfully with The Law of Resistance. It's not possible to work with The Law of Allowing and The Law of Resistance at the same time, as they are polar opposites.

Negative emotions, which you want to steer clear of, are emotions such as:

• Desperation

• Anger

• Longing

• Emptiness

Here's the thing, you can't hold something captive in your energy field, charge it with negative emotion, and expect it to manifest in a positive way. It doesn't work like that. Energy is attraction based—and like attracts like—aka The Law of Attraction.

When you attach a negative emotion to what it is you desire, and hold it captive in your energy field, you create the opposite of what it is you want.

This happens because what you really want is a positive outcome, but deep down you're afraid of a negative outcome. This fear creates the negative scenario over and over in your head until THAT thought becomes believable! Until that thought becomes your reality…

UNIVERSAL LAWS

70% of people have a much easier time accepting a negative outcome as a possibility over a positive outcome as a possibility.

The problem with negative emotions is they're charged with can't have, not possible, won't, don't, anything mirroring a negative outcome. When you charge a thought with negative emotions and attach it to your desire, what do you think is going to happen? You are charging your thought with, "not going to happen"… end of story.

When you learn to work with The Law of Detachment, it's the best way to keep yourself from accidentally charging a thought negatively, because you have separated yourself from the outcome. When you separate yourself from the outcome, it is a million times easier to keep your emotions in check.

The Law of Detachment makes it a lot easier to charge a thought with a positive emotion, thus allowing a positive outcome.

If you cannot learn to work with the Law of Detachment, it most certainly will cause havoc in your relationships with people and with money flow. Working with this law requires you to maintain some healthy aspects, such as:

49

1) Individuality—Thinking differently than those around you.

Maintaining a perspective which is more positive in nature and not automatically going to the worst possible scenario (breaking old thought patterns). You must also maintain individuality in relationships with other people.

2) Balance—Maintaining balance between the spiritual and physical realms.

Super important! Also keeping balance between your individual self and who you are as a person and other people. This helps you to understand that you don't need a relationship in order to be happy and productive.

3) LETTING GO—Letting go is incredibly hard for people to do; however, learning to let go will be one of the most beneficial things you will ever do for yourself.

When you let go, you relinquish the need for control …

What would your world feel like if you released the need to control other people and what they were doing, and you just let go? The responsibility was now off of your shoulders, and you're solely responsible for yourself and the things that you do. Ah, doesn't it feel nice? Why?

Because when you are trying to control a situation or an outcome of a situation that involves other people, you are working with resistance.

How do I know this? Because no one ever has to take control of something that is in the state of allowing, when something or someone is in the state of allowing, it's flexible and ever changing. When situations or people are in a state of allowing ,they become adaptable. When you are trying to control a situation or a person or a person's behavior, the amount of energy it takes is exhausting. The worst part is ***control is an illusion;*** you will never be able to control anything, any situation, or anyone without consent. So in actuality there is no control, only consent!

When you let go, you are no longer forcing things to happen (pushing), you relax into a state of allowing (receiving).

When you're trying to force something to happen, you're working against the Universal Laws. Things don't like to be pushed. When pushed, energetically things tend to remove themselves or push back. You cannot push things into your life; the outcome is unfavorable to everyone and everything involved. Why?

Because anything being pushed is in a state of resistance, and when you are in a state of resistance, there will be friction.

When you relax into a state of allowing, then you begin to work with the Universal Laws. There is no resistance, there is no friction, there is only flow. When you allow yourself to *be in the flow of things*, your energy begins to "draw in and attract" instead of "push out and repel." This allows you to draw into your life things that you wish to happen effortlessly. Allowing things into your life feels fantastic! It feels natural…

When you let go, it allows your energetic river to flow freely.

When you let go, energetically you allow things to flow in and flow out of your life freely. There are no stagnant ponds of energy in your system. This is so beneficial because it means there's also a consistent flow of new energy streaming into your life. Energy that is fresh and clear, your system needs this replenishment for nourishment and for growth. A consistent energetic flow also replaces any old, toxic energy, with new, vibrant energy. It allows your system a way to maintain a clean environment.

When you let go, you welcome change and let your resistance down.

Many people resist change because they know what they currently have, and they think, "What if it gets worse?" They never tend to think, "What if it gets a million times better?" So they resist change with all of their might. Change is inevitable, and there are so many variables to any situation, things that have never even come across your radar. Since change is inevitable, resisting change doesn't stop it from happening; it only makes you feel more uncomfortable while it IS happening. If you stop resisting change, things may not turn out so bad. In fact, you may be pleasantly surprised! Change promotes growth and growth is a good thing. Resistance causes things to break or shatter.

When you let go, you break attachments.

Breaking attachments to something or someone can be incredibly freeing, and energetically you will feel so much lighter! When you are trying with all of your might to hold onto something or someone, you must consistently project a certain amount of energy outward, over and over again, in order to maintain the attachment. This takes a huge amount of effort on your part, especially if the attachment is primarily one sided. You must, in fact, double the amount of energy you would normally send out, because unless the energy is reciprocated, it will die out. In order to maintain this type of attachment, you are either knowingly or unknowingly committed to not letting it die out. Attachments do not promote growth, people use them to try and fill a spiritual void in their life. A spiritual void will never be filled with an attachment; your attention will only be temporarily diverted from it.

When you let go, you allow wasted and toxic energy to die out.

When you focus your attention towards any kind of drama going on in your life (which is extremely common), when you talk about it, discuss it, or give your opinion about it, you are energetically engaging the drama. When you engage, or reciprocate in any way, it is like throwing fuel on an energetic fire, so to speak. Then, in many instances, you can watch this energetic fire burn out of control and injure innocent people along the way.

When energy is sent out or focused in your direction, it can only maintain itself for a very brief time, unless (this is important) ... it is somehow engaged upon.

If you are ever around negative people, and they direct a negative comment or action your way, let it go. Do not engage this behavior in any way, shape, or form. These are battles that are never won, they only appear to be won when someone disengages himself or herself from the battle. This is exactly what I am suggesting you do, disengage and let it go. If you do not disengage, anger, bitterness, and resentment, all of the things that come with engaging in this type of behavior, will then park itself in your energetic body. When these types of negative emotions park themselves in your body, they will then manifest in your cells, energetic or otherwise. Many times this is where manifestation of illness occurs.

Energy that is focused upon you or in your direction has to have some energetic reciprocation or it will just die out.

By all means ... let it die out!

Universal Law #7
"The Law of Abundance"

The Law of Abundance—There is more than enough in the Universe, nothing is limited.

This law is the second most popular law (next to *The Law of Attraction*), but the one law that the majority of people have the most trouble believing in. Even when they say they do, deep down they wonder how it's physically possible.

The Law of Abundance dictates there is an abundance of all things, because there's a limitless supply of Universal Energy.

• Every manifestation stems from Universal Energy, and since this supply is limitless, this law dictates there are no limits when it comes to creating anything. Thus creating abundance.

• People have trouble believing in this law because they have trouble grasping exactly what it means, because from a physical standpoint, it makes no sense.

• We are consistently bombarded with limits. We hear things such as, "There's an oil shortage, and the Earth's resources are running out, the economy is getting worse, jobs are scarce and hard to come by…They only print so much money!"

From a physical perspective, if you take ten things and divide them up equally between five people, there are no more things. But from a Universal perspective, there is an abundance of these so called ten things, and when and if the need arises, ten more things will most certainly appear or more appropriately, be created. And so on and so on!

The Universe works differently. There's an abundance of everything. In other words, there are no limitations. We are limitless! Our greatest desires can be fulfilled in ways that we never thought possible!

From a Universal perspective, all things are possible, always.

As creators of Universal Energy, we have the power to create...well, anything! When we are born into our physical existence, not only do we lose sight of the Universal aspect, but we also become fascinated with material things, or physical manifestations. The issue then becomes, our soul's desires and our mind's desires come into conflict.

What we truly desire and what truly makes us happy to the very core of our soul and our being has nothing to do with physical things, yet this is where our focus lies.

For instance, most people wish for these four things:

1) More freedom.

Many people wish they had more time and more freedom to do whatever it is that brings them joy, such as golf, fishing, seeing friends and family, or traveling the world.

2) Time to be more creative.

Creativity fulfills your soul because it's directly linked to the spiritual side of yourself. The more we utilize our creative side, the more we become aware of our spiritual bodies. This promotes a natural balance between our physical and spiritual bodies and that feels good to us.

3) To explore and adventure.

We're all natural explorers and adventurers. Our soul craves it and our mind puts a cork on it, and then justifies all the reasons why we shouldn't do it. But the longing to explore and the deep desire to learn and see new things still exists underneath it all. Things like discovering a new town, new food, a different mall, or the world, fulfills us to the core of our being. We're here to learn, discover, and experience!

4) More love.

Everyone wishes to have a love in his or her life. They wish to be in a relationship, to feel more love, and even give more love. Yet somehow life seems to dictate a lot of rules on how we divvy out our love to one another.

These four things are all "soul desires" and they are felt very deeply to the depths of our souls. Yet the primary focus tends to be from a physical perspective. *Money.* People train themselves to believe, *if I had more money I could have all of these things…More time, more freedom, I could have it all!*

The consensus among most people is money can and does, in fact, buy you all of these things. The *belief* then becomes, if you have enough money, you no longer have to work so you can enjoy having more free time to be creative, explore, and experience more love as you become more desirable as a significant other.

So you must gather as much of it as you can in the hopes that some day, you'll have gathered enough, which actually creates a bigger problem… when is enough, enough?

If and when money alone becomes your primary focus, a number of things happen:

1) Desperation sets in!

Panic, fear, and worry will eventually creep in and jump right up into your lap, with no intention of moving! To make things worse, it likes to fling doubt at you left and right. The economy is bad, no one is making money, people are losing jobs and houses... You could be next!

2) Misdirection occurs.

Money becomes even more of a focus, you must get it before everyone else does! This is a classic example of misdirection. Instead of focusing on what it is you really want, time, freedom, being creative, etcetera, you focus on money in hopes of buying all of those things. Worst mistake ever! Money doesn't buy you those things. Who exactly do you write a check out to when you want to buy more time? What about freedom? Is it the same person? Silly when you think of it that way, isn't it? We are all allotted the same amount of time every day to do with what we wish. How you choose to spend your time is up to you.

3) Your vision becomes limited and frustration begins to linger.

When people become desperate for money, they begin to go left brain instead of right. They want to follow instead of lead. They try and walk the path of another and if it doesn't work out, they get frustrated. They analyze and seek out who's making the same kind of money they believe they're capable of and they head that direction. This is important to understand, so let me repeat myself. People head the direction, not to what it is they truly desire, but to what they view as "most achievable" for themselves at the time. *In other words, they settle...*

4) You lose faith.

What happens when you settle? You begin to lose faith. You lose faith that your dreams and desires will ever be within reach.

So what's a person to do?

Don't follow; lead.

Don't walk the path of someone else; find your own way. Follow desire, not money! Let me be specific:

• Most people follow money, don't do that.

• Most people see what works for someone else and they try it, don't do that either.

If it's working for them, it's most likely because it's THEIR soul's desire. When it doesn't work for you, it's because it isn't yours! Do you know who followed their souls desire and not money? The Donald Trumps of the world, Richard Branson, Justin Bieber, Steve Jobs, and Sam Waldon. These are only a few people, ones whose names you know. But there are millions of people out in the world who are extremely well off and have free time to do exactly what it is they love to do, who you don't know! You know what they and the NR (new rich) have in common? Two things:

• **They did what they loved first; money came after.**

• **They don't view the world the same as everyone else.**

They don't think inside the box! The NR don't believe in limitations. They consistently test the boundaries and have a strong belief in creating and doing the impossible. They believe in abundance!

UNIVERSAL LAWS

They live in a different world. In their world, anything is possible. In their world, anything can be created. In their world, there IS abundance. When fulfilling your soul's desires becomes the primary focus in your life, what happens is something magnificent! You naturally begin to gravitate and line up with energy that will take you towards what it is you desire. You naturally begin to relax into The Law of Allowing and manifestation begins to happen.

It's where you are supposed to be.

It's where it feels good.

It's where anything is possible!

Universal Law #8
"The Law of Intention"

The Law of Intention—Directing energy as intention is the first step of creation and desire, which results in manifestation.

This Universal Law is greatly underestimated! Not enough people pay attention to this law, even if you forget everything else you learn in this book, this is one chapter I highly recommend you pay very close attention to.

The Law of Intention dictates Universal Energy can and will be directed by intention.

• Universal Energy is directed by your mind, your thoughts, and your thought patterns.

• The Law of Intention and The Law of Action work together, in tandem, because intention is energy which is directed and focused by some type of action taking place. When coupled together, these two Universal Laws become a powerhouse!

• **This is one of the most powerful laws, if not *the* most powerful action law of all the Universal Laws. (The Law of Love being the most powerful non-action law).**

UNIVERSAL LAWS

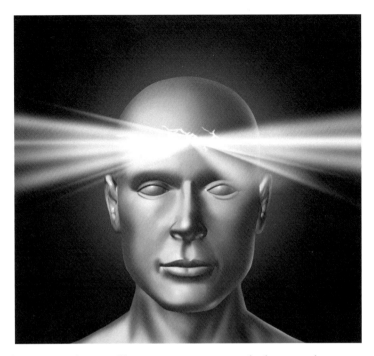

What does intend actually mean? Most people know what it means in essence, but what does it mean energetically? What happens?

It means to "direct the mind" or "to have in mind a purpose or goal" with the intention of a specific outcome or desire.

When you place an intention, two things happen:

1) Energy is directed.

When you intend to do something, you have specifically directed your mind and focused your thoughts in the direction of a certain outcome. You have directed energy to form in a certain manner and manifest in a certain way.

2) Confidence and belief become a huge factor in the equation.

When you intend to do something or set the intention of a certain outcome, confidence and belief become a huge factor in the equation. Because with intention, usually comes determination, and with determination your mind begins to gain a powerful focus and perspective on how your intention will become a reality.

The more you focus upon a desired outcome with determination, the outcome then becomes a probable reality. This is where confidence and belief begin to take over. As this focused thought (intention) is then coupled with confidence and belief…your intention begins to harnesses an incredible power.

You cannot harness a more powerful way to direct Universal Energy than when you have established a belief behind the direction of your thought or intention to do something.

In other words, when you truly set the intention to do or accomplish something, and it's coupled with a true belief that it can be done, you become unstoppable! You become like a powerful wall of energy that is focused in the direction of manifesting an outcome.

You become a Universal powerhouse!

The part of this law (and other Universal Laws) which confuses people, is they fail to realize how truly important *belief* is. It MUST be present. Without belief, the powerhouse is not so powerful.

In order to achieve most things which you desire in life, you must start with some sort of intention. How do you start?

Give Universal Energy a required destination!

Most people don't really give themselves, or Universal Energy, a required destination. Ever!

- They just assume they have no control over the destination.

- They assume that life just happens and they must learn to adjust to how it unfolds.

- They assume that Universal Energy just knows where it's supposed to go, so they don't give it much thought.

- They don't direct the energy anywhere!

This is the biggest mistake ever for two reasons:

1) You've become a victim.

You've become a victim to life, the economy, the weather, the government, your job, your boss, your kids, and your location, etcetera…

How horrible does it feel to think that any one of those things has an impact on how your life goes?

It feels awful!

But it's also untrue, unless of course, you believe it to be true. The only reason you'll ever feel this way is because you don't have an understanding of the Universal Laws. When you don't possess this knowledge you can feel very helpless.

- You don't understand the power that you hold.

- You don't understand the power that you have when it comes to creating the life you desire.

- You don't understand that in order for Universal Energy to manifest in a way that works for you...it needs to be directed!

Giving direction is really important. Imagine this; let's just say you wanted to open a business. You don't know what type of business yet, but you do know you want to be a business owner. You happen to meet up with an investor who sympathizes with your desire and sees your potential, so he's offered to supply you with start up money and a staff to help your business become a reality. This investor has no desire to help you figure out what it is your business should do, only the desire to help you to achieve your goal. You and this investor agree that after ten years, the investor will pull out and leave your company to thrive on its own, as you've both agreed it's a good amount of time to have a successful business up and running.

Now imagine that your new staff shows up on Monday morning, eager to learn and ready to help with this new business. When they arrive, they ask, "What would you like us to do?"

"I'm not really sure yet," you say, realizing you haven't made much of a plan.

They say, "All right, well, what business are we in?"

To which you reply, sort of puzzled, "I don't really know, I haven't given it much thought yet." You now realize your only goal, up until this point, was to become a business owner, which technically you are. But now what?

The staff, now equally puzzled, asks, "How are we supposed to know what to do?"

Suddenly it comes to you. "I want you to help make me a successful business owner!" you gush with a smile on your face. Then you direct them to get started on that right away and let them know you'll be back to check in on them in the morning.

This makes absolutely no sense whatsoever!

Ten years go by and you have become a victim of this horrible staff who did not make you a successful business owner! Why didn't they know how to achieve that? This brings us to number two.

2) Without direction, Universal Energy just flows around with no particular job.

You have a very incredible resource at your fingertips, which many fail to utilize, or even fail to acknowledge that it exists! So this energy (your staff) flows all around with no particular job…

Was it the incapable staff that made the business fail? No.

Was it the absence of much needed help? No.

Was it the economy, the government, your neighbor, the taxes you had to pay, or your location? No, no, no, no and no!

Was it the lack of direction? *YES!*

You're the business owner of your own life and the staff is the Universal Energy which flows in and around your energy field each and every day. In order to direct Universal Energy, there has to be some type of intention set. This intention should then be followed up by action. This scenario would've gone much different had it gone like this.

Your staff shows up on Monday morning, eager and ready. They ask, "What would you like us to do?"

Your response is, "I'm not really sure yet."

So they say, "All right, well, what business are we in?"

Thinking for a minute, you contemplate some ideas and ask yourself, *what is it that I desire? How is it that being a business owner benefits my life?* You get an idea; you want a business which has some longevity. Something which will support you well after ten years. So you say, "Well, I would like a business which would bring me in some residual income. Let's start by researching those types of options and then narrowing it down to one or two."

"Perfect." Your eager staff beams. "We'll get started right away."

Do you see the difference? Even though you're not entirely sure how things are going to unfold (leaving some things up to Universal Energy) you have now given a direction in which to flow. That's a huge difference.

It's also very important to make sure that you set an intention for your desires when it comes to money and love.

If you set no intention, then don't expect different results than what it is you're currently experiencing. If you're happy with the situation you're currently in financially speaking and in your love life, then great, no need to change. If you're not, you can start by asking yourself these questions.

1) Am I happy with my current situation?

Are you happy with your current financial situation? Are you happy with your love life? I don't like to have people even ask themselves this question when it comes to their finances because most people will say, "Not really, you can always use more money, can't you?"

This is where most people *must alter* their perspective when it comes to money.

Especially if you feel you're not happy with your current situation. Stop looking at money as a tangible object, which you can hold, or touch, like paper or a piece of furniture and ask yourself:

- What would I do with more money?

- What am I currently lacking in my life?

- What do I *feel* like money could or would buy me?

- More time? (Don't have to work.)

- More freedom? (Take a vacation.)

- More fun? (A Jet Ski.)

When you figure that out, then you can move on to number two.

2) What do I wish to be different in the future?

This is where I want you to think of as many things as you wish, as long as it's not a material item. Even if you're thinking a bigger house, then you really wish for more space. If you are thinking of enough money to quit your job, then you really wish for more time or freedom.

What most people wish for is not more money; it's for more of what they think the money can buy them.

Once you start separating your soul's desires from material things and recognize your desire to achieve a certain feeling internally, such as a desire to have more time, more fun, more love…then and only then, have you passed a major hurdle when it comes to understanding Universal Laws.

Universal Law #9
"The Law of Action"

The Law of Action—Action must be taken in order to result in manifestation.

This law can also be a huge blocker for people when they learn about visualizing and The Law of Attraction, because they don't learn about The Law of Action. It's not taught and it's not properly understood. If people don't understand its purpose, it can be very easily dismissed.

The Law of Action dictates that Universal Energy needs to be put in motion in order for a manifestation to take place.

• Which is why The Law of Action and The Law of Intention work in tandem. When you place an intention of a certain outcome, action MUST take place in order for a manifestation to occur.

• Action kickstarts the process of energy in motion.

• Most of the time, this is not a problem because when you have an intention to do something, action is involved. It's part of the intention or the movement forward towards the goal which you hold in your thoughts or your mind.

UNIVERSAL LAWS

Many times people only learn about one component of the Universal Laws, they learn about...

Visualizing.

• They learn how visualize and feel a certain outcome through visualization.

• They learn about The Law of Attraction and how important visualizing is to get what it is they desire.

• They learn how to visualize in order to trick themselves into believing.

• *But they fail to learn about The Law of Action.*

So why is action important?

Action is the state or process of acting or doing.

No manifestation will take place without The Law of Action, period!

That would be like trying to grow a plant (manifestation) without having a seed (intention), and then actually planting the seed (action). It's not possible!

There must be a chain of events that takes place in order for the manifestation to occur. Many times a plant will grow if you just plant it. Even if you put it in crappy soil, or don't water it enough, it can, and sometimes will still grow. But if the seed is missing, NO PLANT!

There are no variables here if the seed is missing, there's just no manifestation!

You can visualize the plant growing all you want and it's not going to happen unless someone brings you a plant or a seed…but even in those instances, the seed is still provided. There is some type of action taking place.

The Law of Action works in harmony with so many other laws and the degree of the action doesn't even have to be massive, it just has to take place! Let's take love, for instance. You will not increase your chances of finding love if you never take action to do so. You can be the best visualizer on the face of the planet, and believe with all of your heart that someone is out there for you. But if you never take any action, such as leave the house or accept a date, you may have to settle for your dream date literally in your dreams!

UNIVERSAL LAWS

Now let's talk about money. Even for people who win the lottery, some type of action has taken place, they bought the lottery ticket!

It may have been small, but there was some type of action that took place. Always think of it this way:

Action is energy in motion.

The Law of Action is energy which you are actively directing by some type of motion or movement.

It doesn't have to be a massive movement of energy; movement just has to take place. The degree can and will vary.

Four Important Facts About The Law of Action:

• The Law of Action works in tandem with most all of the other Universal Laws.

• No manifestation will take place without The Law of Action.

• Action is energy in motion, which is a key component to The Law of Attraction.

• When utilizing The Law of Action, the action itself can be subtle or massive. The simple act of energy in motion is all that's needed.

Universal Law #10
"The Law of Cause and Effect"

*The Law of Cause and Effect—Every action
has a reaction or a consequence.*

This law is fairly simple to understand since most people have been taught all of their lives about the consequences of their actions, especially when they were young.

The Law of Cause and Effect dictates that for every action there is a reaction or some kind of response.

• Understanding physical consequences can help you to understand Universal consequences. The only difference is in one instance you can *see* how a consequence unfolds and in the other you may not, but the concept is still the same.

• An action or event will produce a certain response to the action in the form of another event (aka effect or consequence).

• Imagine it like the domino effect. If one gets knocked over, there are several others in the area which are going to be moved or touched somehow, causing some sort of chain reaction.

UNIVERSAL LAWS

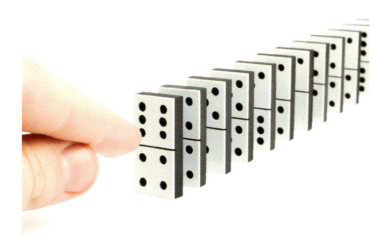

There are some important things to remember when you're learning about The Law of Cause and Effect. Basic things which you might already know, but let's do a quick recap as to refresh your memory.

Five Basic Things to Remember When Working with The Law of Cause and Effect:

• Energy occupies all space; there's nowhere it does not exist. It makes up everything you can see and everything you don't see.

• Energy occupies everything, it cannot be created or destroyed, it just simply exists.

• It forms and reforms when it's focused upon and directed.

• When manifestations occur, *it's energy in movement.*

• When energy is forming or reforming (manifesting), it will have an effect on the energy in the surrounding area, causing the surrounding energy to have a reaction…The Law of Cause and Effect.

For instance, let's talk about emotional energy. This is something which people direct often (and don't even know it).

Emotional energy is energy which you can't see, yet you can certainly *feel* it.

Imagine you're having a bad day. In the middle of this day you end up having lunch with a friend who always seems to have a positive attitude and an upbeat personality. The waitress who brings you your lunch has a really warm smile and wonderful presence about her. What tends to happen in situations such as this?

Being in the presence of people who are emitting a positive attitude and warm behavior will transform most of the energy surrounding them.

More often than not this will have a positive effect on your day. However, the opposite can also be true. When people are having a bad day, they tend to snap at everyone in their vicinity. Many times one person can affect many other people and their attitudes in a very negative way. In both instances, The Law of Cause and Effect has taken place.

For every action (The Law of Action) there must be a reaction (The Law of Cause and Effect).

Now let's talk about what you can see—physical energy. Let's say you have a bucket of water and you put your hand inside the bucket. The water must go somewhere, so the water level will rise inside the bucket as your hand pushes the water aside. Not much is disturbed really, but there's a reaction or effect which most definitely occurs.

However, if the water level is at the top of the bucket and you put your hand inside of the bucket, the water will certainly spill over onto whatever surface the bucket is sitting on. In this instance, there has been a slightly larger effect on multiple things. The water is now having an effect on the surface the bucket is sitting on. If it's soil, the soil may drink up the water and nourishment is provided. If the surface is wood, the surface may also soak up the water, possibly causing the wooden surface to warp and maybe even grow mold.

Why is any of this important?

Because understanding The Law of Cause and Effect can help you gain a better understanding of *ALL* of the other Universal Laws.

You must understand one of the most basic principles of Universal Energy…that Universal Energy occupies ALL space. Therefore, any movement of energy is going to cause some kind of reaction. *It's going to shift surrounding energies in some type of way.* It helps your mind to perceive what's actually happening. When you simply understand the process of how it all works, it makes things a whole lot easier when consciously working with Universal Laws, because it allows you to see how important your role is when working with them.

Universal Laws work in cooperation with all of the other Universal Laws.

Universal Laws work as a team…it's a team effort.

When you focus upon what your intention is (The Law of Intention) and direct Universal Energy (The Law of Action), what takes place is energy changes and reforms (The Law of Cause and Effect), which then results in a manifestation.

So understand that everything you do and the choices that you make all have an energetic consequence to them, which can manifest as emotional or physical in nature. Some people refer to this as *Karma*, but this law actually encompasses much more than that. It encompasses:

- Creation

- Adjustment
- Manifestation
- Change
- Interaction.

They all can play a role in the movement of energy. Karma is neither more important nor less important than any of these things.

Let's talk about two important kinds of energy for a minute and what some consequences might be:

1) Emotional Energy.

How do you perceive money?

Is it hard to come by?

How do you really *feel* about it (The Law of Vibration)?

Do you believe whenever you get money it flows right out of your life?

This type of perception has a very real effect on your money flow energetically. It causes a reaction (The Law of Cause and Effect) to match your perspective (focus and direction).

Just a simple thought…causes a reaction.

You've placed it out there into the Universe, a direction in which energy should flow; therefore, a reaction is going to take place.

2) Physical Energy.

How do you spend money?

The way you spend money most likely reflects your emotional energy about money. But more importantly:

How you *feel* about money will dictate what you physically come into contact with.

So if and when you decide you want to experience a different effect, outcome, or consequence in any part of your life, *it's important that you understand this effect actually started somewhere else along the Universal chain.*

And this means if change is what you wish for, then it's time to revisit some of the earlier Universal Laws. *You must start at the beginning stages in order to see a different result.*

What I really like about this law is it's like a cheat sheet that will let you know how you're doing with all of the other Universal Laws up until this point. How effective are you really being when it comes to the other Laws?

Laws such as:

- The Law of Vibration

- The Law of Attraction

- The Law of Allowing

- The Law of Resistance

- The Law of Detachment

- The Law of Intention

- The Law of Action

These are all action laws, or laws which you must learn to have an active role with. The other laws are also very important, however, you don't necessarily need to have an active role when working with those laws. In fact, you don't really even need to know they exist, although it will make a difference if you do.

It's like when you learn how to drive a car, you learn all of the rules such as:

When to stop and when to go.

What speeds are acceptable.

When you can pass and when you can't.

What the different lights, signs, and signals mean.

Now imagine what it would be like if you had never learned any traffic rules before driving a vehicle. Or imagine that the first time you started driving a vehicle was in another country, where you were completely clueless to the traffic rules and you had to figure everything out on your own.

This would be very difficult because the training and knowledge that you gain with studying and guidance or a driver's education class can make a world of difference. Just having an understanding of what's happening around you and what your role is while driving in a sea of other cars can help you have a very different outcome (The Law of Cause and Effect).

So consider the knowledge you learn here, as with each law, to be equally important for your journey through the sea of Universal Energy, which you live in every single day. It will help change your outcome.

Universal Law #11
"The Law of Pure Potential"

The Law of Pure Potential—Everything and everyone is one of infinite possibilities.

The Law of Pure Potential is truly underrated, if you ask me. When you understand this law, your perspective can really shift. When your perspective shifts, then your belief system will go ahead and jump on board more easily.

The Law of Pure Potential dictates the possibilities of what a person can become and make of their life are not limited in any way, shape, or form.

- Everything is energy, and as energetic beings, we hold the power to move and direct other energy with NO limits!

- When working with Universal Laws and while directing energy, there are no boundaries, there are only infinite possibilities.

- *The potential of every living person is infinite.*

How can this be? You may wonder.

There are no limits when it comes to what you can create or things you cannot create. The only thing which stands in your way of infinite possibilities… IS YOU.

Three Road Blocks Which Keep People From Achieving Their *Pure Potential*.

- Lack of knowledge.

- Their belief system.

- Lack of focus.

Contrary to what seems like popular belief, your hands are not tied when it comes to what it is you can achieve on a *quantum physics level.*

You're not bound by:

- Where you live.

- How you grew up.

- The people who you know or don't know.

- Your current situation.

You're only bound by your own thoughts and perception (*psychological level*).

That's it!

How did this happen? Years and years of brainwashing and being taught how you have no control over what it is you can become and what it is you can achieve. You've been taught you are bound by some external Universal force which limits you and only the lucky ones break free.

This isn't actually true, and it really makes things quite interesting since the opposite is actually true. This force is not against you, it's actually with you. It's with you working to help you achieve your potential. Everyone always wants some type of scientific proof in order to believe in something.

Where does it state we have no control?

Where's the proof?

Quantum physics states the complete opposite. Why weren't you taught those things?

As energetic beings, we're all working with The Law of Pure Potential, not some of us, but ALL of us.

Now you may find yourself thinking, "Right! I'm no Donald Trump or Richard Branson!"

Who says? How do you know? You're not exactly like them, as they have created their own identity, and their identity is their creation, not yours. But you do have something in common, The Law of Pure Potential.

What do successful people (athletes, entrepreneurs, singers, actors, the wealthy, etcetera) all have in common?

They never bought into the illusion that they were limited in some way.

They believed that somehow, someway, they could achieve whatever it was they set their mind to.

Some people utilize their potential to the fullest while others, well… they settle. They settle for becoming less than, they settle for a life they don't want to live, they settle for average. Lots of people do it. You might be thinking, "It's just the way it is! Look at all of us, we're all struggling!"

Who's all of us? The people you surround yourself with? The people who tell you, "It's not possible. What are you thinking? How are you going to make a living doing that?" You mean those people?

What about all the other people? What about the people who are not struggling? What choices did they make that are different from yours? What's different about them?

They never bought into being average.

The people who settle, buy into being average hook, line, and sinker. That's the difference!

If you want something different:

Surround yourself with different people.

DO something different.

BE DIFFERENT!

People who work well with The Law of Pure Potential *truly* believe four things. They believe:

1) The masses are wrong, life is not supposed to be hard!

They believe you are who you surround yourself with. You are an accumulation of all the perspectives of the people who are in your life most often. Slowly but surely their perspectives become your perspectives. Subtly your energy will shift to match the people you're closest to. In other words, their energy becomes your energy and your vibration will adjust to match theirs.

2) They are leaders, not followers.

People who work well with The Law of Pure Potential don't like to follow the masses.

They're individual and independent thinkers and they don't like to have their thought process conformed by the masses. They respect other people who also have independent ideas, because more often than not, individual thinkers tend to crave growth and like to feed their creativity. They like to try new things and discover new ways of doing things. They're creative, adventurous, and positive!

3) They can be or achieve anything they want to in life. It's just a matter of following their dream.

They truly believe anything can be accomplished when you set your mind to it. They're not easily discouraged, and they like to test the boundaries. The fear of failing might be present, however, the fear of not trying or settling is much greater, so failing is not an option.

4) They ARE different.

And they like it! They don't fit in with the masses and they're very comfortable not fitting in. When you begin to have a better understanding of the Universal Laws, things will change internally for you.

Their internal perspective changes and suddenly they feel...different. They feel different than the masses of people who they might have fit in with previously or sometime before. Suddenly, the things other people are saying and believing don't make sense to them. They begin to question the negativity factor that tends to heavily weigh in on other people's lives, swaying them to do the easy thing, to settle.

Different is good! You don't need the support of the masses. All you need is the strength and knowledge to be different.

People who struggle with The Law of Pure Potential *truly* believe three things. They believe:

1) The masses are a reflection of how the world works, it's proof!

They take the masses as some type of proof of how the world works. Things are hard and that's just the way it is. Look at everyone else, they're struggling, too!

What's really proof is you have a large population making the same decisions and choices. You have the masses all swaying each other's perspective to validate their own situation, proving to themselves and others that it's NOT a matter of choice, it's a matter of circumstance. Well, they're doing a very good job!

2) Things such as location, finances, and the economy keep them from achieving their goal.

They believe they don't stand a chance in this economy. They believe that if they were in a different location, then they might be able to do something different, only they can't afford to move. They believe there are only so many jobs and so much money to go around and they're not one of the lucky ones.

3) They find themselves comfortable fitting in with the group.

They find themselves more comfortable going with the masses and following what they believe to be true, than being independent from the group.

Being an independent thinker allows you to be a target of the masses.
They may judge you and criticize your decisions. Many of these people include friends and family. For some people, it's just too hard to battle all of these people and justify their new actions. How dare they think differently from the group! They also like to feel accepted and like they belong with popular belief and opinion.

These are not facts, these are perspectives. In order to learn how to work with The Law of Pure Potential, you will need to be able to shed old beliefs (and perspectives) and break free of the masses. You will need to want something different for yourself more than you want to be popular.

Universal Law #12
"The Law of Rhythm or Ebb and Flow"

The Law of Rhythm or Ebb and Flow—All things have a rhythm, a cycle, or an ebb and flow.

This law is really unique because you can actually *see* the affect it has had on Mother Earth for thousands of years.

This law dictates that all Universal Energy flows in rhythms or cycles, which has more force at certain times and less force during others.

• These rhythms or cycles are not abrupt in nature, but the flow is fluid with a rhythm or an ebb and flow.

• Mother Earth shows us often how The Law of Rhythm or Ebb and Flow works, we can actually *see* it!

• Cycles have been a vital part of our survival in the physical world since the beginning of time, so The Law of Rhythm or Ebb and Flow is really important to our existence and our growth.

• It has fairly predictable effects (The Law of Cause and Effect) on other energies. Because of this, many of these cycles are and have been charted throughout time. By using those patterns, we can also predict when they will occur in the future.

There are massive amounts of cycles occurring all of the time. Some in tandem with each other and others occur on their own. Here are some cycles which you're probably familiar with:

1) Cycles of the moon.

Full moon, half moon, new moon, blue moon, these things all have an effect on Universal Energy. These cycles affect the earth below and how things grow. They also affect people and the behavior patterns of all things. Many people joke about it, saying things like, "It's a full moon, people are going to be crazy tonight." People who work closely with other people may be aware of these behavior changes. It becomes a noticeable pattern, especially at night.

Farmers have used the cycles of the moon to their benefit for centuries. There's great knowledge that can come with understanding and observing cycles. Farmers use moon cycles in order to help them know when the best times to plant crops are, and even when to harvest crops.

Some fishermen also pay close attention to moon cycles, as it also has an effect on the behavior of the fish (all living things, including animals and fish, respond in different ways to these cycles). They are more active during some times and less active during others.

Cycles of the moon can be a very helpful tool when properly understood. Especially when you learn about how it affects the energies around you.

2) Changes of seasons.

This is fairly obvious, but changes in seasons are also cycles and they do have an ebb and flow to them. Plants and trees change with each season. Animals alter their behavior. They change location, hibernate, grow more fur and shed old coats as they adjust to each new cycle. Even people tend to be less active during the cold winter months and more active in the summer months. Their energy levels are directly affected by different seasons as their bodies adjust to the external effects which are occurring.

3) Tides of the ocean.

People who live near large bodies of water often pay close attention to the tides of the ocean because they can tell a lot by what the tidal pull is doing. The tidal pull is actually directly linked to the lunar cycle. The gravitational pull of the moon pulls the ocean up and down at different times of the day or month. These things all have different effects on sailing conditions and fishing.

4) Calendar years.

These have been charted all the way back into early BC. Calendars are used to help people keep track of cycles, the most famous one recently being the Mayan Calendar, which was used to track different eras, the newest era being the Consciousness Era, a time a spiritual enlightenment. Then of course you have other ones such as the Chinese calendar and our own yearly calendar, which keeps track of seasons, solstices, and moon cycles.

5) Astrological cycles.

Astrological cycles are incredibly important as well because they take into consideration the position and alignment of the planets, then predict the effects those planets will have on many other things based on years of observation and the information that has been gathered. Planet alignment, planetary shifts, and the effects these things have on everything else from other planets, such as Mother Earth, to plants and animals which thrive on Mother Earth shows The Law of Rhythm or Ebb and Flow on a grand scale.

When you think about how everything is really tied together (The Law of One or Oneness) and how so many things affect each other (The Law of Cause and Effect) by a chain of events or cycles (The Law of Rhythm or Ebb and Flow) it's really quite amazing!

- The Universe (planets and planetary alignment) all have an effect on the sun, other planets, and moons (Mother Earth and it's moon).

- Moons have an effect on bodies of water (tidal pulls, and don't forget humans are 70% water), therefore affecting behavior patterns.

It's something our ancestors used to pay very close attention to, but in today's society, it's considered unimportant and less prevalent. While things such as food, water, and shelter have become readily available to us, this information seems…well, unimportant! This makes things much more complicated when you're trying to understand Universal Laws and how Universal Energies work.

It causes a huge information gap between how things really work in the Universe and how people think things work.

- People have a misguided perception that all things are now controlled by money and the tech savvy industry.

- While these things do have an impact in our world today, as do all things that are energy, these things are still dictated by Universal Law.

- Just because we have advanced largely in the technical field does not mean things no longer work the way they used to energetically.

- Energetically, things will never change. All Universal Energy remains the same and bound by the same Universal Laws now as it was hundreds of thousands of years ago.

What has changed?

People are less informed.

- In current times, people acquire knowledge on a need to know basis. This is something which many feel they don't need to know. If and when they feel like they need to know it, they will Google it.

- It's this lack of information which causes a real disconnection between how you think the world works and how it actually works.

Energies and the laws which dictate energetic flow cannot EVER be replaced by technology, devices, or technological advances, it's not possible.

In fact, technology and technological advances will cease to exist without the presence of Universal Energy and Universal Laws. Why should any of this matter to you?

• Because as physical beings, we are affected by cycles and the ebb and flow of Universal Energy.

• It's important for you to understand things which may have a great impact on your life and on the events that may occur, including many things which you cannot see, such as Universal Laws.

• For many people it's easier to bridge the gap in their mind from physical to energetic when they can *see* the effects on the physical world around them.

• When you observe your surroundings and pay more attention to what's happening with the ebb and flow of the world, and the cycles of the Universe, you can actually *see* how it affects the physical world around you.

When you do this, you're observing actual evidence. Evidence of what you've been looking for…evidence that Universal Energy exists.

This in turn helps to *retrain* the way you look at things. It teaches you to have a new perspective, which is imperative to understanding the Universal Laws.

Universal Law #13
"The Law of Polarity"

The Law of Polarity—Everything has an opposite, a yin and yang. Complimentary opposites are part of a greater whole.

This law is one which most people have at least a little bit of knowledge about or most likely they've heard of the concept before because it's not only about having opposites, but about finding balance.

The Law of Polarity dictates that there's an opposite to all things, complementary opposites to a greater whole.

• This is what helps to maintain Universal balance.

• If there were no opposites in Universal Energy, physically or energetically, it would become very difficult to maintain proper balance in the Universe. Things would become off kilter, so to speak.

• As complementary opposites, there's a physical and spiritual component to all things, including yourself! This law helps you to understand what happens if you don't understand or maintain both the physical and spiritual aspects of your own existence.

UNIVERSAL LAWS

Here are some examples of opposites which you are most likely familiar with:

• There is light and there is dark.

• There is day and there is night.

• There is good and there is evil.

• There is positive and there is negative.

• There is happiness and there is sadness.

It's all of these things, small or large, which help to balance the greater whole. You're probably wondering, "Why do I need to know this? Those things are obvious."

Because being aware of why we have opposites can be extremely beneficial in several areas of your life. More importantly, it can be helpful when you're trying to understand this law.

Understanding The Law of Polarity helps you to become more aware when balance is not being achieved.

Three Signs and Signals of Imbalance Are:

1) Things become upset.

Emotionally or physically, things which do not maintain a proper balance will become upset in nature and the energy feels chaotic. This can cause uneasiness and anxiety on an emotional level and create a disturbance, or even destruction, on a physical level.

2) Things do not flow with ease.

This is a HUGE sign of imbalance. I'm not talking about a few instances of difficulty, but more of a "theme" of difficulty. It feels like you're in a losing battle and you're pushing things up hill. When you're consistently having to use force, this implies there's most certainly imbalance present.

3) Break downs occur.

Without proper balance, weaknesses become prominent, and when this happens, break downs will occur…often! The better the balance, the stronger something becomes energetically, which in turn makes things stronger physically, and even emotionally, if and when it applies.

It's also very helpful to pay attention to what it feels like when you're balanced. There are also signs and signals which appear when balance is being achieved.

Three Signs and Signals of What Being in Balance Feels Like:

1) Peaceful.

A calming and peaceful energy becomes very present.

2) Things flow with ease.

And it feels wonderful! Energy is directed with ease and everything around you seems to be working together as if part of a nicely choreographed dance or a well oiled machine.

3) Strength is predominant.

Areas of weakness become isolated and rebuilt to become stronger. Stronger energy will search for areas of weakness in order to rebuild and strengthen those areas as well, allowing strength to be predominant over weakness.

Balance is a really important factor when it comes to maintaining good physical health.

• When balance is mostly achieved energetically, it will transfer through your cells and into your physical state.

• Cells, like all things, are first created from an energetic state and your physical body is constantly creating them. So it's important that cells are created from a state of balance.

Your body creates new cells all of the time to replace old cells. Imagine what happens if and when your body creates cells from a state of imbalance. What do you think happens when you create new cells from a state of chaotic energy?

Creating new cells from a state of imbalance causes weaknesses to become prominent. They are not as strong as other cells.

Now imagine what happens when you create new cells from a state of balance—*the energy, the strength, the peace and harmony forming and creating new cells!*

Do you feel the difference?

It's not important for you to maintain balance all of the time, that's not even very realistic. Without having had imbalance in our life at some point in time, we wouldn't know what it feels like to have balance. It's a good idea, however, to strive for maintaining balance most of the time, or as often as you can.

Universal Law #14
"The Law of Relativity"

The Law of Relativity—Everything has challenges or tests to face, allowing the ability to find strength within.

I'm sure this is not your most favorite law and I have to admit I am not a huge fan. However, this law also has its benefits.

The Law of Relativity dictates that in order to grow, prosper, and evolve, everything must face challenges and tests which allow energies to adapt and find inner strength.

• Plants, people, animals, and even material things such as cars and furniture adhere to this law.

• Throughout the history of the evolution of everything, problems have been met and resolved, thus allowing growth to occur.

• If humans, plants, or things were never challenged or tested in any way, things would become very different.

Just think about it for a minute. If energies were always drifting in a smooth and relaxed state, with nothing ever arising to test our physical or emotional strengths and weaknesses, what would happen?

- **It would eliminate the need for evolution and growth!**

- Energies would never shift or change. There would be no need for it.

- Evolution and growth arise out of necessity for change and adaptation, and there would be no need to change or adapt to anything.

- Evolution and growth is super powerful and important! It keeps energies from becoming stagnant.

- It's also why we are here on this earth in a physical state. We are here to learn, grow, adapt, and evolve…***Spiritually.***

These things all help us reach greater spiritual heights and higher levels of consciousness.

What are the benefits of evolution and growth?

- Finding Inner Strength

- New Discoveries

- Knowledge

These things are really important to our souls on a deeper level. Super important to our inner being and ourselves as part of a greater whole.

When people get really caught up in their physical existence, many times they deny what the soul craves. Many times what the physical self and spiritual self wants will differ.

Your physical self can get caught up in the "physicalness" of the world and all it has to offer. When this happens, your perspective can shift away from your inner self and your spiritual needs and desires—what the soul really craves. The soul doesn't desire winning the lottery, a new red sports car, or a house on the beach. What the soul craves is happiness, freedom, more time, and time to slow down and enjoy life. However, when you become out of touch with your spiritual self, this thin line becomes blurred.

Material things become a primary focus.

Material desires can become a temporary fix for a spiritual void, and in some instances, you might even experience a certain level of fulfillment for a short period of time. This causes confusion because it might seem *as if* your material desire represents what your soul desires, but what's really happening is it's distracting you away from your true desires for a moment, then after a period of time, your desires will resurface again. Very confusing.

So what happens when our soul remains unfulfilled?

Luckily we have The Law of Relativity with tests and challenges to help us find strength within.

I'm sure you're probably wondering how this makes us lucky. Well, this law helps us find a way to get back in touch with our spiritual bodies again. It helps us reconnect with our true self and rediscover who we are on a spiritual level, as a spiritual being. Many times this part of us can become lost or overshadowed by our physical existence.

If and when you can find a way to balance your spiritual self in a physical world, you will find that your physical existence will most definitely benefit. Some amazing things can happen with The Law of Relativity and the tests or challenges you might face. Such as:

1) The Law of Detachment kicks in.

Many times tests and challenges you go through will cause you to realize what's really important to you in your life.

Things such as people, relationships, time, many things which cannot be physically replaced…those things are very precious!

This allows you to detach more from the physical world and from the things in it. Don't get me wrong, physical things are nice, I like them myself! But they're also replaceable.

It also allows you to detach more from a very specific outcome and become less controlling, because let's face it, as long as things always work out best in the end, that's all that really matters. When you're too attached to a specific outcome, you can't always see what's best, or even learn from what's happening at the time. You become too wrapped up in controlling the situation.

2) You face your fears.

Many times you'll face some of your biggest fears. People have many different fears in life such as the fear of losing a job, a fear of poor health, or a fear of growing old.

But the number one biggest fear people have is the fear of dying or of a loved one dying.

When you realize that a physical death in this lifetime is most definitely going to happen and there's not a thing you can do about it (Remember, you will only leave your physical body behind and you will most definitely still exist in the spiritual realm. Energy can only change shape, it can't be destroyed.), *it's incredibly freeing!*

You will continue to exist, with your memory intact of who you are and who you know. You will see other loved ones who have also released their physical bodies and continue to live on in another existence. You will continue to be…well, YOU! When you can really grasp that reality, things will really shift for you.

3) Your perspective will shift.

When you begin to understand things are not as they appear to be, you will begin to realize that you can only see a very small portion of what actually exists in the world and in the Universe.

The Universe is most definitely not controlled by what you can see, but by what you can't see… When you can truly wrap your mind around this concept, it is at that moment you will become very powerful!

You have the power to control many things in your existence, things which you cannot see. These things hold the power to control things which you can see. It's very euphoric and surreal, and very powerful!

When you allow yourself to "see" more of what you can't see, your whole world will become different, and you'll never want to go back.

Universal Law #15
"The Law of Dharma or Purpose"

The Law of Dharma or Purpose—Everything was created with a purpose.

This law I really appreciate. I find that most people have a good understanding of this law when it applies to nature and other things, yet dismiss the validity of it and have a hard time believing it to be true when it applies to themselves.

The Law of Dharma dictates that all Universal Energy was created with a purpose.

• Everything in existence was created with a purpose. The sun, the moon, the trees, the animals, and even you and I were all created with a purpose.

• For things such as trees and the moon, these energies have a very good understanding of their purpose from the very beginning of their creation and they assume their roles flawlessly.

• When it comes to humans, however, things can be much, much different. Why? Because of a little gift we've been given called "free will," and it tends to, well, let's just say, have a mind of its own sometimes.

UNIVERSAL LAWS

As spiritual beings living in a physical world, we tend to play tug of war with different desires (good and bad) in order to learn what our purpose is.

Our purpose was instilled within us at the very beginning of our creation, when we were first created in energy form. In other words, *our purpose started with our spiritual existence, not our physical existence.* When we change into physical form, our purpose never leaves us, it's still very much a part of who we are. It's with us to the very core of our being.

Here are some examples of a person's purpose:

- Teachers

- Musicians

- Humanitarians

- Creators

- Warriors

- Athletes

- Intellectuals

- Farmers

- Leaders

One of our jobs in the physical world is to figure out what our purpose is. Some of you are probably thinking, "Great! That sounds easy enough! How do I do it?" And others are thinking, "I'm 43 years old, if I haven't figured out what my purpose is by now, I don't think I ever will." Or even, "I have a family and a spouse, I don't have time to sit down, let alone find my purpose." (I have written more about this in my book Soul DNA).

It may feel overwhelming for some people. However, it's important to your health and well being when you live in the physical world. Why? Because as physical beings living in a physical world, often you will begin to lose touch with your spiritual self. This will cause you to become imbalanced, just like we discussed in the previous chapter.

When imbalance occurs, it will affect your physical health and your money flow.

It affects your spiritual health and your overall well being. It really affects you on all levels and this can make for a very hard, very long journey here on earth. So finding your purpose is really something you don't want to ignore.

So how can you figure out what your purpose is? You can start by asking yourself some very simple questions:

I am most happy when I'm doing _____.

I am the most passionate about (what subject) _____.

When I was a kid, I used to love to _____.

If I never had to worry about money ever again, I would _____.

If I could get paid to do any job in the world, I would choose to _____.

Most likely you will begin to see a "theme" appear in your answers. It's all about figuring out what it is you're most happy doing in life or what it is you're most passionate about, whether it's watching (whatever your passion is) on TV, participating in or reading about it, therein lies your purpose. It almost sounds too good to be true, but it's not.

Your purpose is intertwined with your passion.

How do I know I'm not following my purpose already? You might wonder. Well there are some very distinct signs you will notice if and when you begin to follow or pursue your purpose.

Three Signs You are Following Your Purpose (or you're at least on the right track):

1) Energies around you begin to work in harmony.

Things which you desire and wish for begin to orchestrate nicely into your life in a way which you did not see coming. Relationships in your life become more harmonious and the ones which are not will fade out of your life, sometimes completely. Timing of everything seems to become impeccable and often things or events become synchronistic.

2) You become fulfilled to the very core of your soul.

This is something you can't get anywhere else but from your purpose. You can't get it from another person and you most definitely can't get it from acquiring material things. It feels like you have struck a harmonious chord deep inside your soul and it feels like you are vibrating in harmony with the Universe. Sometimes people correlate this feeling with being in a "zone."

3) The physical world is no longer so hard to live in.

Things begin to feel easier. Problems seem to resolve themselves without much effort from you. Abundance becomes a reality and you seem to have more than you do less. You begin to trust the Universe more. Things that you need will show up when needed, things such as money, people, or help.

People can have more than one purpose and this is also important to remember. Feel free to pursue different passions at different times in your life. Sometimes it can take years for a purpose to show itself to you in its entirety. You may just be gathering knowledge along the way for quite some time and then all of the sudden, there it is! You understand your purpose completely!

The next hurdle you might have is how to follow your purpose or work with it. Many times when people ask themselves these questions, the problem is not trying to figure out *what* their passion is. More often than not they know what it is right away. *The hurdle becomes their mindset.*

"Yeah, right, how am I supposed to do that?"

"There's nobody who does XYZ and makes a living at it!"

"I'm not good enough to do XYZ. I just love to watch it or read about it."

Don't make this about money! Remember, your purpose is tied to your spiritual self and spiritual fulfillment and nothing else.

Wrong mindset:

- *Your purpose is a way to make yourself a ton of money.* —This is wrong!

Right mindset:

- *Your purpose is way to fulfill yourself on a soul level, which in turn allows money to flow into your life.* —Aaahh, now you get it!

Money cannot and will not flow into your life *effortlessly* when you have not found your purpose or fulfilled yourself on a spiritual level or on a soul level. If you remain unfulfilled, it will take great effort to draw money into your life, period!

This is why The Law of Dharma or Purpose is not only important for maintaining your spiritual wellbeing, but it's also important when living in the physical world.

Find your purpose and follow it with the passion you already have. Don't tell yourself a hundred reasons why you can't do it. Challenge yourself to find ways in which it's possible. Because anything's possible!

Universal Law #16
"The Law of Giving and Gratitude"

*The Law of Giving and Gratitude—The Universe
dictates that you must give in order to receive.*

This law is actually understood quite well by many so I won't spend a ton of time on it.

The Law of Giving and Gratitude dictates that you must give in order to receive, as old energy is replaced by new energy.

• The Law of Giving and Gratitude keeps energy moving and helps to keep energy from becoming stagnant.

• It keeps the ebb and flow of the Universe going and often it will help you to find within yourself Universal Energy in its purest and most powerful state…love.

• The Law of Giving and Gratitude many times works in tandem with The Law of Love, making a very powerful team!

People worry so much about what it is they are getting or receiving in their life and worry so much that they will never *receive enough* in their lifetime that they forget to or DON'T WANT TO give. Often they don't even give gratitude for what they do have, because they don't have enough!

So they become desperate to receive...

What happens if people wish to receive more and more and never give in return?

It stops the flow of energy!

Universal Energies are in constant motion; it's the way it works with the ebb and flow of the Universe. When you never give and only receive, you become what's essentially **a hoarder of things or energy.** And remember all things are energy. Many times people do this because they are afraid. *Afraid of what?* You might wonder.

Of never receiving anything else in the future to replace what they've given out, emotionally or physically.

They're afraid there's not enough abundance in the world to go around, "So you must take what you can get! And keep it if possible." People will do this in order to calm their own anxieties of never having enough. So then what happens?

It becomes a self-fulfilling prophecy…

Because when you do this, you're consciously trying to stop the flow of Universal Energy. You're keeping energy stagnant in your field. And when you stop energy (spiritually or physically) from *flowing out of your life,* you will also stop energy from *flowing into your life.*

The natural state of Universal Energy is to be in motion and to flow.

If you try and stop the flow or dam it up, it will behave like a river. It will not stay with you, but it will make a new path and flow around you. Energetically, you'll force things to do the opposite of what it is you really want.

Things will not flow towards you, but around you.

When you give to others and find gratitude and appreciation, it will benefit you in several different ways:

1) It will keep energy moving into your life.

Energy that goes out will then be replaced by new energy which flows in. When you don't have something in your life which you desire, there must to be a way for it to flow into your life. If you stop movement, you will stop the flow, and without flow, it's not possible. So it's important to allow the flow of Universal Energy to come in and out of your life, without trying to hoard or stop it. This way new energies will flow in as well.

2) It helps you to become more positive.

Finding gratitude is a great way to shift your perspective towards all things positive. Finding gratitude means to find things to be grateful for, and you can't be grateful without being positive. This essentially raises your own vibration energetically. When this happens, it allows you to tap into a very powerful Universal Energy.

3) It allows you to tap into the greatest power of all. Love.

When you allow yourself to search for positive thoughts and allow yourself to find gratitude, you consciously direct energy through your heart chakra. When this happens, your energy becomes charged with love. There is no greater power in existence than love. When you direct energy from your heart chakra, it's like Universal Energy on steroids. It's pure, it's powerful, and it's pretty unstoppable.

The Law of Giving and Gratitude really works hand and hand with our next Universal Law, which brings us to our next chapter, The Law of Love.

Universal Law #17
"The Law of Love"

*The Law of Love—Love is Universal Energy
in its purest, most powerful state.*

This law is really special. It's a state of being and you can feel it to the very core of your soul. The effects this law can have on people is quite amazing, but only when it's in pure form with no conditions attached.

The Law of Love dictates that love and positive feelings are Universal Energy in its purest and most powerful state.

• Universal Energy, when charged with love and positive feelings, can actually change molecules and affect how they interact with each other.

• It's considered a non-action law as love is a state of *being*.

• You can *feel* The Law of Love activate through your heart chakra.

• **It's Universal Energy in its purest state.**

Here's some important information that will help you understand how Universal Energy and The Law of Love work together:

1) As spiritual beings, people charge energy all of the time...with emotion.

Emotion is a very powerful component when it comes to working with Universal Energy. Universal Energy will always remain energy, but as energy, it can also hold a charge. People are able to charge energy simply with their *thoughts and feelings* towards something or someone (emotions). Although there are thousands of different emotions, it really comes down to two primary factors, are they negative or positive in nature? Thoughts and feelings will always fit into one of these two categories.

If you attach a positive thought to something, the energy surrounding that particular thought will hold a positive charge. If you attach a negative thought to something, the same thing will happen, the energy surrounding that particular thought will be charged with a negative feeling or charge. This is why you will be unsuccessful if you imagine a particular outcome, couple it with disbelief, and then expect something positive to happen. Universal Energy doesn't work that way. It can't, because of The Law of Correspondence (next chapter). When you charge a particular thought negatively, the outcome will follow Universal Law, and the outcome will transform negative in nature.

Here are some examples of what type of emotion gives off what type of charge:

Positive Charge

- Love
- Happiness
- Hope
- Belief
- Excitement

Negative Charge

- Hate
- Anger
- Sadness
- Disbelief
- Fear
- Worry
- Anxiety

It's really important to be aware of the feelings you're surrounding your thoughts with. In fact, it's imperative, especially when you're directing energy.

2) Universal Energies are also attracted to and collectively move towards other like energies.

Negative energies are attracted to other negative energies and positive energies are attracted to other positive energies.

That's why it's imperative.

This applies to all energies such as things, thoughts, and people. It's why people who tend to be negative in nature are usually surrounded by other depressed or angry people, and people who are more positive in nature tend to be surrounded by other happy, upbeat people. Same thing goes for thoughts.

Your negative thoughts will seek out other negative energy and manifest from that state.

Not good! The good thing is your positive thoughts will do the same thing and manifest from a positive vibration.

So what do you think would happen if you used what you now know about The Law of Love? What if you paid very close attention to your thoughts and actions and charged everything with love? You would be sending out the most powerful purest energy in existence and it would seek out other "like" energy and manifest from that state.

Everyone wants to feel loved.

Love is a major component when it comes to interpersonal relationships; family relationships, platonic relationships, or intimate relationships. Love plays a major role. Love raises your vibration and opens your heart chakra. Love is also energy, and as energy, it must follow the laws of the Universe. This is important, especially for those of you wishing to have more love in your life. Energy needs to keep flowing or moving. With flow and movement, energy is consistently being replenished. With replenishment, old toxic energy is moved out and new vibrant energy replaces the old. Whatever energy you put out must be replaced (unless you resist).

Six Helpful Tips When Working The Law of Love:

1) Love has healing properties!

Love is a very powerful! It has an amazing effect on other people as well as your spiritual and physical body. The more you love, the more you activate your heart chakra, which is a very important chakra to exercise. The heart chakra is tied to your higher consciousness, your vibration, and your intuition. It also helps balance all other chakras in your system. The more love you offer, the more you will also receive.

2) Never place conditions on your love.

Love unconditionally. Love as energy takes on a different form when you place conditions on your love. When working with The Law of Love, your love can't be offered with anything other than *love in pure form*. When love is offered with conditions, the energy is no longer powerful, it's no longer activating your heart chakra, it becomes something else that you are sending out into the Universe, something else that will flow back into your life. It becomes toxic love; love that is toxic to your system and others.

3) Keep love pure.

Love cannot be held hostage and it's not a form of manipulation; love is just that, love. Love in pure form cannot be held hostage. What do I mean by that? Holding love hostage is when you don't like someone else's behavior, so you decide not to "reward" him or her with your love. In other words, if they behave a certain way or do something you don't agree with, you make sure not to show them any love. That's not love in its pure form; that would be toxic love. You see, love is not trying to manipulate someone else's free will and the choices they make; love is loving someone regardless of the free will choices they make!

4) Love unconditionally.

When offering love, it's only offered in its purest form when it is offered unconditionally. Will people you love do things you don't agree with? Yes. Will people you love make mistakes? Yes. Will people you love even make bad choices? Yes. That's why we're all here on earth as spiritual beings, to potentially do all of these things. Then hopefully we learn and grow as a result of doing all of these things. To never encounter any disappointment from yourself or others is unrealistic. It's most important for you to love unconditionally, regardless of choice, and regardless of mistakes, because we're all human, and as humans we sometimes make mistakes.

5) Only receive pure love.

Pure love can't be used as a manipulation tactic, but toxic love can be. Don't mistake anyone who wishes to change who you are or your behavior in exchange for his or her love, as love in pure form. In fact, that's not love at all, it is just manipulation in disguise.

Pure love is offered unconditionally, with no strings attached. There are no guidelines you must follow, or potential you must live up to; you are just loved for the simple fact that you exist!

6) Love more.

Self explanatory....

Universal Law #18
"The Law of Correspondence"

The Law of Correspondence—The Universe, or reality, cannot contradict itself or its laws in any way.

This law can be fairly simple. Everyone knows what laws are, they're a system of rules which regulate the actions of something (in this case, Universal Energy). These rules cannot be altered!

The Law of Correspondence dictates that all Universal Energy is governed by Universal Laws and these laws cannot contradict themselves under any circumstances.

• The Law of Correspondence also dictates there are no exceptions when you are dealing with Universal Laws.

• Each law has a very specific purpose and they will not be altered for any reason at any given time.

• Universal Laws and Universal Energies have some really distinct qualities to them. As long as you remember these qualities, you will not need to remember each and every law in detail.

Think about it this way for a minute. Imagine how the city works everyday with vehicles driving every which way. People are going to work, dropping their kids off at school, running errands, and just plain having fun. What would happen if there were absolutely no traffic laws? What would happen if there where no traffic signs or signals and yet the same amount of people were out and about each day? Can you imagine the chaos? How easy would it be to get from your house to the grocery store? Well, the same thing would happen if there were no laws to govern energy. And since ALL things are energy, you can imagine the craziness that would occur.

So if you can't figure out a way around them, you might as well understand them.

• Universal Laws are laws which govern energy and dictate the movement and flow of energy.

• If there were no laws to dictate how energy flows or behaves, our world (even as we know it in the physical realm) would feel very chaotic in nature.

• Under no conditions can these laws be altered or changed.

UNIVERSAL LAWS

I'm not going to spend too much time on The Law of Correspondence, as it's really pretty clear. But if you remember these five things, it will help you immensely!

Five Key Points to Remember about Universal Energy and Universal Laws:

1) The power lies in what you can't see, not it what you can see.

2) Everything is energy.

3) Your happiness level or *vibration* plays a very powerful and important role.

4) Universal Laws *are not* dictated by Physical Laws.

5) Flow is really important when working with Universal Energy.

Universal Energy must follow laws. You and everything that you know of in existence is made up of energy. Without laws, there would be chaos. Universal laws are very real and very important to your life in the physical world. Understand them, respect them, and learn how to work with them. The quality of your life depends on it!

What Does It "Feel" Like When Working With Universal Laws & Manifestation?

I wanted to touch upon this subject so you'll know what it feels like when you're working with Universal Laws and manifestation. Then at least you can have some frame of reference on what to strive for in the future. Books often talk about how to manifest your desires but they don't talk about *what it feels like* when you're doing it correctly. So needless to say, it's important and helpful for you to understand what it feels like, because it helps to give you a sign that you're on the right track. Should you be feeling these things all of the time if your manifesting correctly? No. But you will feel them often, and these very feelings (when you pay attention to the signs and signals) will help you know when you're on the right track!

1) It feels like you're in a "zone."

Anyone who's ever played sports most likely knows what I mean when I say this, but for those of you who don't know what being in a zone is, I will explain it to you. *It's when you achieve a certain level of higher consciousness.* It implies increased focus and attention, which seems elevate performance. It's a very euphoric feeling, and a huge boost of confidence in whatever it is you're doing accompanies this focus. You seem to have an understanding with the Universe and you "just know" that you will not fail. When you're in a "zone," you can feel everything flowing perfectly through your spiritual body and you *just know* you can accomplish anything. There's a kind of natural high that comes with being in a zone.

When you are in a zone, this higher state of consciousness will actually activate your upper chakras. Some of you may feel even feel them. You might feel a tingly or open sensation in, near, or around your fourth, fifth, sixth, and seventh chakras. For those of you who are unfamiliar with chakras, these four chakras will run near your spine, anywhere from between your shoulder blades all the way to the top of your head. See the diagram below:

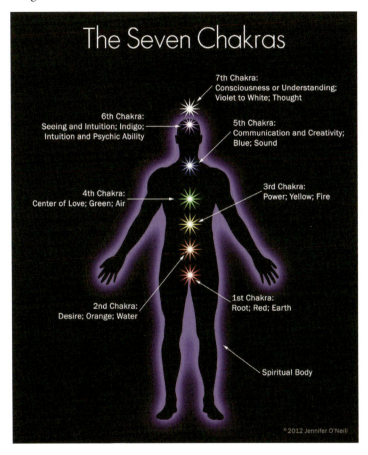

Just to be clear, chakras do not run down the center of your body, of equal distance to the front and back of your physical body, (this is where many people think their chakras are because of the way they appear on diagrams). Your chakras are actually located near your spine and near the back of your neck and head.

2) Things become simpler.

Things become simpler, everything around you seems to flow with ease, and nothing is resistant. Things don't *feel* difficult, they feel like they will work out just fine, and they do. Things will feel easy. Relationships will feel easy, work will feel easy, everything will feel like it's flowing with ease.

3) Your desires tend to appear right before your eyes.

As you raise your vibration and advance your manifestation skills, you will notice that the world around you will begin to respond to your thoughts. Usually you will notice this with everyday things, because those are the things that grab your attention the quickest.

For instance, I was with my brother not long ago as he just moved to my area, and he was asking me about a particular construction company. He wanted to know if I had heard of them before. I've lived in our area for many years and I told him I'd never seen this company before. Not ten minutes after we'd had this conversation, we were heading out on a coastal drive. As we took a right turn, we happened to drive right by a house with the exact construction company he was looking for. We both looked at each other and I thought, "Weird!"

This particular day also started out cloudy and I said, "Well, I know you wanted it to be sunny, but we've had a long winter and it looks like it might rain."

He said, "No. I want it to be sunny, just wait." After about a twenty minutes into our drive, the sun came out and it proceeded to get hotter than it had been in months.

He also wanted to see some whales, so we stopped at a costal lookout, and lo and behold, there they were, about fifteen of them! This was kind of surprising, as it was the end of whale season. We went to another lookout and saw even more whales. He said, "This is so cool, but I really wanted to see them breaching." Now I've been in Hawaii for many years and I've seen a lot whales, but from shore, you don't see them breaching very often. Well, it only took about two minutes before the first one breached. We just laughed. But it went on, groups of them even, for like half an hour. I'd never seen so many whales breach, ever!

3) Things become synchronistic.

The world around you will become synchronistic. This is when the experience of two or more events that are apparently unrelated or unlikely to occur together by chance, come together and occur in a meaningful manner.

I have a very good example of something like this that happened to me the other day. I was researching something and found a particular person who I thought could be very helpful. I found this person's website and blog, yet I searched all over and could not find their contact information. Nothing! After awhile, I gave up and thought, "Well, I guess it wasn't meant to be." The very next day I woke up and checked my email like I always do and I noticed a familiar name attached to an email in my inbox. I thought to myself, "No…it couldn't possibly be!" But it was. The very person I was trying to contact had emailed me! I couldn't believe it! She didn't know me and there was no reason for her to know I was trying to contact her. We are not even in the same industry, yet she contacted me on a completely unrelated subject and so I was able to ask her what I wanted to ask her in the first place.

Just remember that when you are first learning how to properly understand and work with the manifestation process, these *signs or signals* can seem very subtle at first. In fact, most of the time when these things start happening, people actually brush these signs and signals off completely and label them as *coincidence* in their subconscious. Worst thing you can do!

Don't ever brush off signs and signals from the Universe…write them down!

This is something I strongly suggest people do when they are learning how to work with the Universal Laws or manifestation. *It helps to retrain your brain.*

Writing these "coincidences" down does a few different things:

1) It documents proof.

This proof is for you and no one else. You're trying to *retrain* your subconscious and your subconscious loves proof. When you write things down, it helps turn a sign or signal from the Universe into physical proof (documented on paper). Proof which you can refer to over and over again. It's a diary of what happened when. Also, the proof will just keep piling up. You may start with one or two things, but the next thing you know there will be pages and pages.

2) You will see how powerful your thoughts are.

After you do this for a while, you will begin to notice a correlation between your thought process and these signs and signals. Whether you're having a good day or a bad day, when you write it down, its not too hard to see a pattern. Your awareness will heighten for sure and you will pay more attention to what it is you're thinking.

3) It trains your mind to search for success.

This is actually a fun game to play, writing down signs and signals or coincidences from the Universe. ***It will train your mind to start searching for a "connection" between these signs and signals instead of figuring out how to explain them away.*** (Something you're already trained to do, and most likely you're quite good at it.)

* Please note that this is a process. You have spent many, many years trying to block out signs or signals from the Universe, so you have to learn how to tear down the very wall you have spent many years building. However, as your awareness begins to heighten, (and it will if you are consistent) these signs or signals will become anything but subtle. But it takes time, so be patient.

Manifestation Exercises

I have an exercise which I use daily even to this day. In fact, I started doing it for fun as a way to help raise my vibration. It was an experiment at first; however, when I noticed the impact it was having on my life, I immediately took it more seriously and began to use it to retrain my subconscious.

You see one of the secrets most people don't know, including those who teach about manifestation, is there's a particular time every day that is OPTIMAL for raising your vibration and reprogramming your subconscious.

It's the time right before you fall asleep.

The reason for this is:

1) This is when you align yourself spiritually.

When you put yourself into a dream state, or even right before you drift off to sleep, naturally, without you even knowing it, your spiritual body will begin to align itself with the spiritual realm. Since you're a spiritual being, you must do this every day in order to live in the physical realm, you will die without sleep, and this is why. It has been proven by the scientific community that your physical body does not need sleep in order to live, your physical body gets enough rest during the day while driving, sitting, or lounging around. However, your spiritual body has to "plug in" to the spiritual realm in order to maintain your physical existence. So naturally your spiritual body raises its vibration as high as it will go in order to plug in to other spiritual dimensions (you probably know it as dreaming). When you plug in and fall asleep, all of your "resistance or subconscious blocks" subside, allowing you the most optimal time to manifest and reprogram.

2) You will wake up with the same vibration you fall asleep with, and this is important when manifesting.

So if you go to bed upset or with a low vibration, you will wake up that way. If you go to sleep happy and content, or with a high vibration, you will also wake up that way. And your morning's vibration will not only set the tone of your day, but it will have a big impact on how you manifest things. You will either manifest things from a negative or positive mindset. We want you to work with a positive mindset as often as you can.

Here's something which I find very interesting. Do you know what most people usually use this most valuable "reprogramming" time for?

• Rehashing their day. (And it's usually not in a good way, as we are *trained* not to stay in a happy place for too long, but to be responsible and solve problems before they arise… You know, tomorrow.)

• Worry and stress about tomorrow. (I have to pick up the kids, do the laundry, give a presentation, have a meeting with so and so, get up early, get the car fixed, etcetera.)

• Worry and stress about their future. (How am I ever going to be able to retire? How am I going to get a new car? How am I going to pay for college?)

Think about it—what do you think about before you go to bed at night? The kids? Work? Pay very close attention, and never, ever spend the time before you fall asleep worrying or stressing about ANYTHING! All that does is bring up fear and worry.

So here is what I teach my clients to do and what I do myself every day.

Manifestation Exercise

1) Commit to thinking positive thoughts only!

No fear or worry allowed! *The time before you fall asleep should forever be a worry free zone!* Do you need to stop worrying forever? Well, that would be ideal, but not very realistic. But give yourself a break from it consistently every day. You can worry in the daytime tomorrow.

2) Get in touch with the child inside. You know the one who believed in Santa Claus?

Find that part of yourself again, it's there, it's a part of who you are. Remember what it felt like when you were little and you believed in a world that was much more magical. Pull that person to the surface! See the world through a young person's eyes and allow yourself just a few minutes to relax into the perspective that anything is possible.

3) Search your thoughts and ask yourself…

- What would my ideal life be like?

- What's currently missing from my life?

- What would I do if I won the lottery for 12 million dollars?

This last question is really fun and it can really help with this exercise. What if you never had to worry about finances again, what would you do? What would your life be like? What would you do every morning? What would the rest of your day be like? Where would you live? Would you do yoga on the beach? Would you travel?

4) Spend time creating your "fantasy world" every night.

If you do this every night, what will happen is it will become your happy place. Somehow it becomes more real and it really starts to become your own little fantasy world. You might spend your time in your fantasy world doing yoga on the beach each day. If you do, the beach will become more and more familiar each time you visit. If you spend your time in this world building your dream house, over time you will become very familiar with this house. You will be able to add things to it over time.

5) Stay in your "fantasy world" until you fall asleep.

This is very important so as not to be distracted by real life issues—you can deal with them tomorrow!

When I started doing this, like I said before, it was just for fun, but then some very real things began to happen.

So I decided to take it to the next level.

Advanced Manifestation Exercise

Don't try and skip the first manifestation exercise and go right to this one, because it won't work correctly. You will still have too many blocks from your subconscious.

Once I had this fantasy world down, a funny thing happened. It became my happy place and a very relaxing part of my day. Up until this point, I didn't really look forward to going to bed. Not because I wasn't tired, but because I had gotten into the pattern of stressing about what happened that day and what was going to happen tomorrow. This became apparent to me when nighttime became enjoyable again.

So I decided to try something new. Why not see if I could have more control over the things I worried about? Now each night it would usually be something different, as you experience different things every day, which causes you to have different anxieties. So here's what I did.

1) I would go into my fantasy world.

After you do this exercise for months, your subconscious will automatically direct you there as it becomes your routine. The cool thing is your subconscious doesn't know the difference between this world and your physical world. Since there's no difference, you can experience some of the same excitement as if it is real, unless you force yourself awake so you can remind yourself it's not real.

2) I would stay there until I could feel the "zone."

When you do this over and over, you will begin to find yourself in what I like to call a "zone." You are feeling happy and euphoric, enjoying your "world."

3) I would recall a worry I wish to be resolved.

JUST FOR FUN, I would imagine the best case scenario of how I wished my worry would be resolved. For instance, if I was worried about paying a bill, I would imagine I was in the future, whether it be a day or a month in the future, and how good I felt that the bill was already paid. If I was worried about doing a talk somewhere, I would fast forward to after the talk and imagine talking with people afterwards who were smiling and very happy to have been a part of the audience, that I had given them something of value. If I was worried about how I was going to get something done (because it felt overwhelming), I would fast forward and imagine that somehow, somewhere, I either received information or help arrived at just the right time and things felt very simple in the end, not hard.

I also did this because *I was trying to retrain my subconscious to see a positive outcome consistently and no longer have negative thinking on autopilot.* I find it interesting how most people's subconscious has been trained to automatically produce the worst-case scenario to any problem.

It's literally automatic!

Even just imagining a better outcome seemed to help eliminate a ton of worry. That's when weird things started happening. Those scenarios started to turn out the way I wished them to. Consistently!

So I took it a step further…

I wanted to see how far I could consciously take manifesting a better outcome. Did it have the same effect or could it have the same effect if I did it during the daytime, in the morning, perhaps? So here's what I did:

Manifestation Meditation

This meditation exercise is designed specifically to help you manifest more of a stress free environment. It's a very effective exercise, which should be done at least once a day, preferably in the morning, but you can do it in the evening for the next day if you need to. It's especially helpful when you're stressed out.

1) Find a quiet place where you will not be disturbed.

2) Sit comfortably in a chair or in an upright position. Place your hands to your side and feet flat on the floor. Don't cross your hands, feet, or legs.

3) Close your eyes and concentrate on your breathing. Slow your breathing to a relaxed state.

4) When your breathing is rhythmic, concentrate on relaxing all of the muscles in your body.

5) Imagine your day from beginning to end. Start with the minute you're done with this meditation and go through the events of the day. (Not minute by minute, but cover the overall events which you wish to go smoothly).

6) Visualize how smoothly things go, from traffic, to work, to dinner. Play each event through your mind like you are creating a movie of it ahead of time. When you've gone through the events of the day…here's the most important part…

7) Imagine yourself at the end of the day smiling and feeling happy. Imagine looking back on your day and thinking to yourself, "Wow, what a great day!" FEEL it from the center of your chest. Feel the happiness when you think about what a great day you had.

8) Bask there for awhile. Milk out the happiness feeling for as long as you can, feel your chest expand with happiness. Enjoy it…

Remain in this state until you feel a sense of completion, then release this image into the Universe.

I like to do this every morning, although many people enjoy doing this exercise at night. There's no right or wrong as to the time you spend, you should adjust the time to whatever feels right to you.

Six Common Blocks That Keep You From Manifesting Your Desires

In closing, I wanted to address some issues, in case you find yourself running into some hang-ups along the way. I went ahead and made a list of the most common blocks people encounter when learning how to work with Universal Laws and manifest their desires. What do I mean by blocks? It's just like it sounds, a list of six things that can keep you from being able to discover your ability to manifest your desires. I have also given solutions for each block, as I want you to have all of the tools you need to make this a successful journey.

Block #1

You Don't Have Enough Information

This is very, very common. If you don't have enough information on how the Universal Laws work, it's next to impossible to learn how to manifest your desires. Even if you do a successful job, without verification, or the proper knowledge of signs to look for to help you verify you're on the right path, you will question yourself and brush it off. What I have noticed from years of teaching is that students who came to me were not getting enough information about the manifestation process in its entirety. There are so many things you need to be aware of, important things, and many of these are being left out. I am confident that I have covered all of those things here in this book. If I have left something out and you have a question that has not been covered, please go to my website and e-mail me; contact information will be at the end of the book. I will be happy to answer those questions for you.

Block #2

Your Belief System

Your belief system is something which you have spent many years working long and hard at creating; so don't be upset if you can't seem to break down these barriers overnight. You have been trained your entire life to think one way about how the world works. Just think about it, if people can't see how something works, such as Universal Laws, they tend to immediately brush it off as impossible. People need to be able to *see* things in order to believe in them, otherwise it's hard for them to wrap their mind around *the impossible*. The idea that you could learn how to manifest your desires has quite a magical feeling because it's quite magical! What have you been *trained* to think your entire adult life about anything that gives you a magical feel? Well, you see where I am going with this. It's more important, now than ever, to challenge and restructure your belief system.

Block #3

Materializing your desires

When you are wishing for cars, houses, and boats, instead of time, freedom, and happiness, this will cause you problems when it comes to learning how to manifest. When you materialize your desires, you've missed the whole point of how the process works. Material things can and will manifest into your life if what you seek is more on a spiritual level.

When learning how to manifest, your main goal should be finding balance—feeling good on the inside and spiritual fulfillment. It's not only important, but imperative for you to learn how to nourish your soul before you'll ever be able to manifest your desires consistently. This doesn't mean you need to become a yoga guru or become a vegetarian. It means you need to get in touch with your soul's desires and you can only do that by keeping your true self and who you are intact. All it takes is a shift in your perspective and how you're looking at things.

For instance:

• Physical desire: Mansion or larger house.

Soul's desire: To have more space so as not to feel so cramped.

• Physical desire: Relationship.

Soul's desire: Fulfillment and to feel like I have a purpose.

• Physical desire: Sports car or boat.

Soul's desire: More excitement and more fun in my life.

- Physical desire: Money or winning the lottery.

- Soul's desire: More time and freedom to do more of the things I enjoy!

When people wish for something in their life, it's always to fill some kind of spiritual void. However, people don't take the time to understand their own desires and why they wish for something. So understand your desires! If you have a material desire, that's totally fine, just ask yourself, "What void will this fill in my life?" I had a client who once wished for a Maserati (material desire), translation was success + more fun (soul's desire). When they finally "got it" and understood the process, what happened? Their desire became success + more fun = enough money to buy a Maserati. Their business took off and it became a reality in less than one year.

Block #4

Fear

Part of the process of understanding how to manifest your desires is letting go of fear. If you truly understand Universal Laws and how the world really operates around you, it should help you with this. Most people fear:

1) Death or dying.

I hate to be the bearer of bad news, but we are all going to leave this physical world sometime, we can't stay here forever. I am certain you already know this. However, understanding Universal Laws and how energy actually works (all things are made of energy, including yourself), this should help to lessen this fear since you should also understand energy can't be destroyed, it can only change shape.

2) Not having enough.

Again you should understand that there will always be enough (The Law of Abundance) and it can never not be so (The Law of Correspondence). If you are having problems with not having enough, then most likely you are still *brainwashed* with a poverty mindset.

3) Failing health.

Your spiritual health will dictate your physical health. However, there's always a time and place to use western medicine. As long as you do your best to maintain and care for your energetic and spiritual body, your physical body will respond.

Block #5

Unhappiness & Negativity

If you are unhappy in your life, you need to figure out how to fix that first. Unhappiness and negativity both bring your vibration down immensely. If you don't know how to do that or where to start, you may want to start with another book I wrote called "The Pursuit of Happiness: 21 Spiritual Rules to Success." You may also want to try and eliminate as much negativity in your life as possible. Many times things don't necessarily emit negativity, people do. This can be another hurdle which can be quite overwhelming, but entirely necessary. I also wrote a book on that for this very reason, "Energy Vampires: How to Deal With Negative People." It has also proven quite helpful for people who need help in this area.

Block #6

Giving Up Too Soon

Like I mentioned before, it takes some time to retrain your brain and learn how to work with the Universal Laws and the new knowledge you have acquired, and it will most likely not happen overnight. You'll need to be committed to learning how to find balance between the spiritual and physical worlds for a period of at least six months. Don't try it for a couple of days or even a couple of weeks and then say, "It's not working!" If that's your plan, I will save you some time here and tell you now, you are right, it probably won't work. Your success depends on knowledge (gained here), practice (what you learned), challenging your beliefs (this part is actually fun and you should do this all the time, anyway), being consistent, and being patient. These things take time, so don't give up too soon. I have taught thousands of people how to manifest their desires, and I have a huge success rate. And if you follow these things, I have no doubt in my mind that you, too, will be successful!

About the Author

Spiritual teacher and best selling author Jennifer O'Neill is devoted to helping others learn how to live a happier life. Through manifestation and her own psychic abilities, she helps others learn how to develop their own spiritual gifts through readings, classes and workshops. The focus of her writing and teaching is to simplify the process of using the spiritual tools and gifts you were born with in a way that fits into your everyday life.

She is the author of several books and has developed a virtual spiritual learning center called Keys to the Spirit World, where you can get find lot's of free articles, find books, listen to radio shows, as well as take classes and webinars.

Jennifer is also one of Hawaii's top psychics and the leading expert in the field of Soul DNA. She has spent the last twenty years as a professional psychic and spiritual teacher helping people all over the world learn how to develop themselves spiritually.

Twitter:

@hawaiipsychic

Facebook:

https://www.facebook.com/JenniferONeillAuthor

Website:

www.keystothespiritworld.com

Other Books By Jennifer O'Neill

Energy Vampires: How to Deal With Negative People

Intuition & Psychic Ability: Your Spiritual GPS

Keys to the Spirit World: An Easy To Use Handbook for Contacting Your Spirit Guides

The Pursuit of Happiness: 21 Spiritual Rules to Success

Soul DNA: Your Spiritual Genetic Code Defines Your Purpose

Soul DNA the Ultimate Collection: Your Spiritual Genetic Code Defines Your Purpose

The Book of Love: Relationships and Dating

Intuition & Psychic Ability: Your Spiritual GPS

Inspirational Quotes

CPSIA information can be obtained at www.ICGtesting.com
Printed in the USA
BVIW12n1407130818
524336BV00023B/123